Reignite Your Spark!

Simple Steps to Extinguish Stress and Go from Burned Out to Fired Up

CARLA WHITE

Reignite Your Spark™
ISBN-10: 9781775370208
Publisher: *Carla White*™
Designer: Helen Scarth, Stuf² Incorporated {*www.stuf2.com*}

To order this title, please visit:
www.carla-white.ca

To connect with Carla, please email:
carla@carla-white.ca

In Loving Memory of

Dale Cameron Crisp
March 8, 1965 - May 18, 1979

Cassidy Victoria Crisp
December 2, 2001 - December 26, 2014

"What moves through us is a silence, a quiet sadness, a longing for one day, one more word, one more touch. We may not understand why you left this earth so soon, or why you left before we were ready to say good-bye, but little by little, we begin to remember not just that you died, but that you lived. And that your life gave us memories too beautiful to forget." *Author Unknown*

Endorsements

"*Reignite Your Spark* is an insightful and relatable book, in which Carla recounts her journey from the darkness of depression to the light of love and laughter, in which she shares the powerful and meaningful lessons she learned on her search for happiness and fulfillment. The book is easy to read because Carla writes with such awareness, vulnerability, and humor."

Jack Canfield, *Co-author of The Success Principles™ and the Chicken Soup for the Soul® series*

"Carla White has lifted a veil of silent suffering for many, women who struggle with feelings of self-doubt about being a mother, a wife, a friend, a woman in general. From seemingly random, chaotic mental and emotional fragments and shards, she has created a masterpiece of the human experience."

Danne Reed, *International Best-selling Co-author of Fashionably Late: Real Life Stories of (Finally!) Showing Up, Founder and CEO of Fashionably Late Productions*

"*Reignite Your Spark* is truly a book to love. Carla White shares a powerful story of personal transformation. This book will change the way you show up in the world. It is inspiring and uplifting."

Teresa de Grosbois, *#1 International Best-selling Author of Mass Influence, 4X Best-selling Author, International Speaker and Founder of the Evolutionary Business Council*

"*Reignite Your Spark* is a must read! Carla White shares a powerful resilient and relatable story, providing the reader an excellent

Endorsements

guide to reducing stress and strife in life. It is moving and entertaining all at the same time. This is a great guide for the workplace and home."

Charmaine Hammond, *Best-selling Author & Professional Speaker*

"Carla White shows you how one story can heal a heart after years of pain. She guides you with laughter and tears through suffering and challenge into your beautiful magnificence. I recommend this book."

Deborah Sandella, PhD, RN, *#1 International Best-selling Author of Goodbye Hurt & Pain, 7 Simple Steps to Health, Love and Success*

"I found myself laughing and crying right along with Carla's journey. This is a delightful book full of wit and wisdom, and I really didn't want it to end! There's no way you can read this book and NOT feel more enlightened by the time you finish."

Tina Dietz, *Creative Business Expert, Audiobook & Podcast Publisher, Owner of StartSomething Creative Business Solutions*

"This book is what I would call "good" medicine, using grace and humor to help us all see that no matter where we are starting from, we each can live a happy, fulfilled life. I enjoyed the supportive tugs on my heart and mind while reading Carla's uplifting stories and practical tips of life."

Anita Sanchez, Ph.D., *Author of The Four Sacred Gifts: Indigenous Wisdom for Modern Times, Co-author of Success University for Women I and II, and Founder of Sanchez Tennis & Associates - leadership and organization development firm*

Endorsements

"Carla White's book, *Reignite Your Spark* is authentic, transparent and evocative. Anyone reading this book will question how they are showing up for life… find their way to living happier, healthier, and more meaningfully by following Carla's lead. She models how to bring our best selves into any situation - both the triumphs & the challenges with humor, grace, and courage."

Kathy Sparrow, *Self-Leadership Expert and Message Strategist, Co-author of Ignite Your Leadership: Proven Tools for Leaders to Energize Teams, Fuel Momentum, and Accelerate Results*

"*Reignite Your Spark* is my story and your story as well. Carla's quest to find herself by losing and finding her voice is one we can all relate to. This book was easy to read because of the fun nature in which Carla communicates. It's inspiring and empowering to know we can all find our true happiness when we are willing to silence ourselves long enough to listen. A book I would recommend to all my friends."

Miriam Laundry, *Award-Winning Author, Speaker and Guinness World Record Holder™*

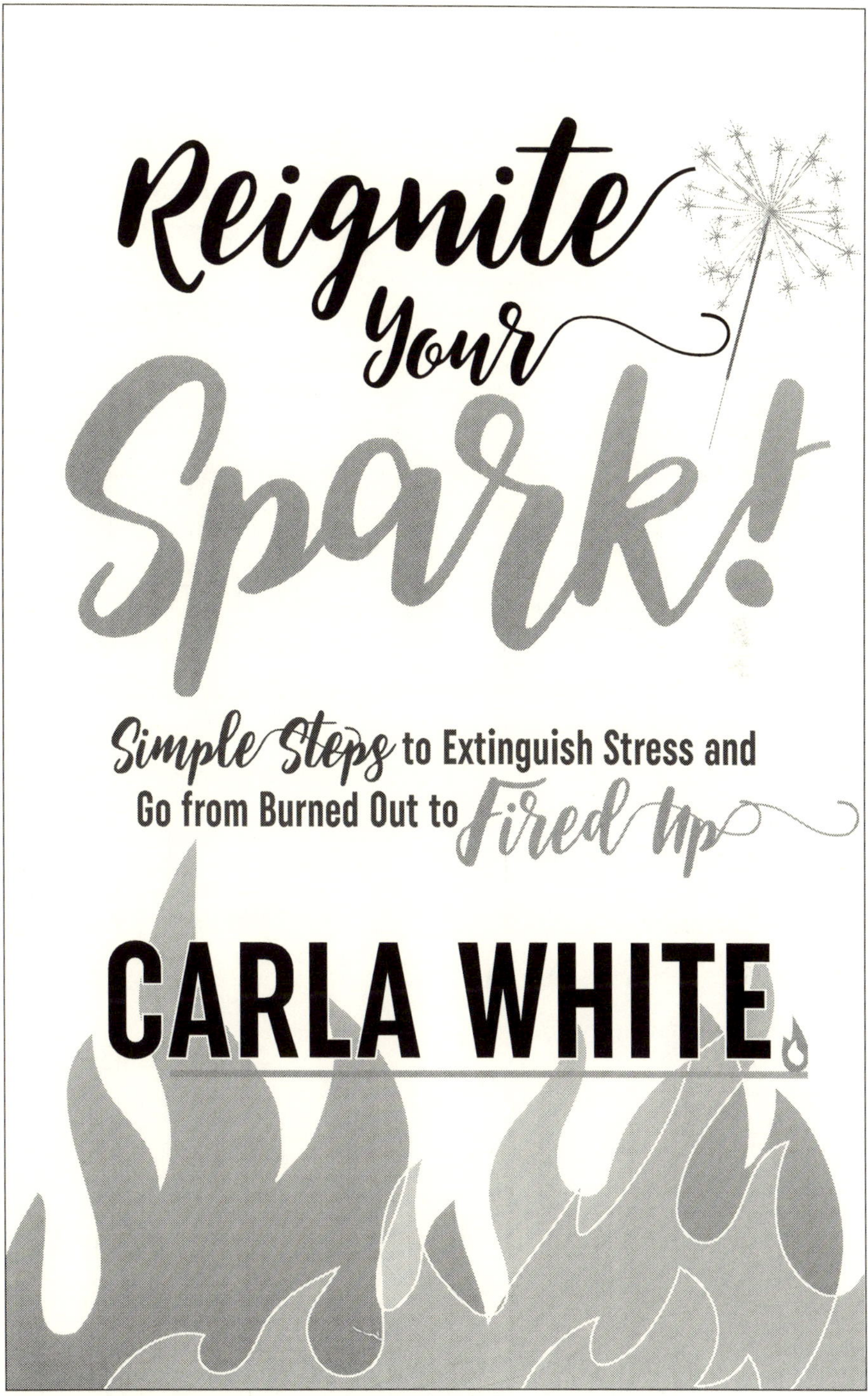
Reignite Your Spark!
Simple Steps to Extinguish Stress and
Go from Burned Out to Fired Up
CARLA WHITE

Disclaimer

I have tried to recreate events, locales and conversations from my memories of them. In order to maintain their anonymity in some instances I have changed the names of individuals and places, I may have changed some identifying characteristics and details such as physical properties, occupations and places of residence.

Although I have made every effort to ensure that the information in this book was correct at press time, I do not assume and hereby disclaim any liability to any party for any loss, damage, or disruption caused by errors or omissions, whether such errors or omissions result from negligence, accident, or any other cause.

Contents

Foreword

I first met Carla White as one of my students at my annual Breakthrough to Success training.

Carla knew of me long before we actually crossed paths. She had seen me speak in her home province in Canada and was inspired to become a motivational speaker, but as often happens with heartfelt dreams, she had let other things get in the way of fulfilling her destiny. However, many years later she rekindled that dream, which led her to my work, and to subsequently graduating as a Canfield Success Principles Trainer. Carla stood out from a lot of my other students because she showed up as a fun-loving, engaging, and entertaining storyteller.

For years she has been coming back as a member of my team, helping others to also become Success Principle Trainers.

Now she has gone and written a book. *Reignite Your Spark* is an insightful and relatable book, in which Carla recounts her journey from the darkness of depression to the light of love and laughter, in which she shares the powerful and meaningful lessons she learned on her search for happiness and fulfillment. The book is easy to read because Carla writes with such awareness, vulnerability, and humor.

Carla seamlessly weaves her personal stories and perspective into a compelling chronicle of her time at a ten-day Vipassana meditation retreat. This holds personal significance for me since I too had a profound experience of deep life-changing insights at a Vipassana retreat thirty years ago.

I am pleased to say that my describing that experience to Carla was an impetus for her to attend her retreat. Through her honest sharing of this silent and deeply powerful spiritual experience, she provides the reader with easy-to-understand concepts that are applicable to overcoming any obstacle you might face in life.

Whether you are struggling with dissatisfaction and disease, are in search of your own answers, or you simply want to achieve more love, joy and peace in your life, this book will inspire you and guide along your own journey.

Let Carla's stories and discoveries serve as a catalyst to take the time to deeply examine your own beliefs, transcend your limiting thoughts, and rise above and move beyond whatever might be holding you back from being your authentic, true self and creating the life you truly want.

Jack Canfield

Co-author of The Success Principles™ and the Chicken Soup for the Soul® series

Introduction

Something was missing.

Rather than a sudden flash of insight, the awareness came over me, slowly and progressively, that something was missing in my life, yet I was clueless as to what it might be.

I was struggling to feel fulfilled, energized, and enthusiastic about my life. In reality, I was tired—more accurately, I was exhausted—not from a lack of sleep, but from what I now know was a weariness of my spirit. I equated it to slogging through thigh-high black mud that chilled my bones and made every step forward such a huge effort that most times it was easiest to not move at all, to stay stuck right where I was. And then, at long last, came the dreaded clinical diagnosis.

Depression.

Being diagnosed with depression was a blow to the strong and independent woman I strived to be. It certainly didn't suit the confident, composed superwoman image I was trying to portray to the outside world. At the same time, the label provided a sense of relief. Suddenly, I had a reason to feel the way I did. Despite having a fortunate and terrific life, I was sad, disappointed, and dissatisfied. While I resisted at first, eventually I gave in to my doctor's suggestion to be medicated for my mental illness. For ten years, antidepressants helped me get through the day, merely coping with, rather than thriving and enjoying, the rigors of being a stay-at-home mother, a wife, and a woman.

I had what could be considered a pretty normal life, growing up on a farm near Consort, Alberta, the kind of place where everyone knew your name—as well as your parents, grandparents, and even great-grandparents. I experienced the usual teenage struggles and joys of fitting in and making plans for a fabulous future life. So it was a bit of a surprise to me when I found myself in the "picture perfect" life, and was not gloriously happy, ecstatic to bounce out of bed, seizing each moment of the day.

I knew something had to change—and somehow, I knew *that something* had to be me.

My decision to stop taking the antidepressants was easy. Following through was the challenging part. It was a gradual process, and my doctor supported me throughout, but I had waves of panic about how I would manage without my "happy pills." It turned into a tsunami of questions—*now what, why me, how do I cope, what do I do?* I was seeking answers from health professionals, and in seminars, courses, and self-help books. I believed the solution to my quest for happiness and contentment was out there somewhere. *Wherever "there" is.*

One day, while surfing the web, I stumbled upon Jack Canfield doing a webinar about writing a book. This was not my first exposure to his work. Nearly twenty years prior, I had been so inspired when I saw him speak at a conference that I announced to my family that I wanted to be a motivational speaker just like Jack.

Incidentally, have you ever had an inspired moment where you envisioned yourself in a different life, doing something you loved to do, and were so excited and enthusiastic about it that you said it out loud to someone... and immediately felt the dream dissipate as that person expressed doubt or suggested an obstacle?

When I told my family that I wanted to be a motivational speaker, I was presented with the following well-intentioned challenges to my idea:

"You can't be a motivational speaker. You haven't done anything great or interesting like write a book, win a gold medal at the Olympics, survived or overcome a big obstacle."

"You need to have a message. What's your message?"

And that was all it took. At the time, I said nothing in response and silently chose to allow their doubts and questions to become an insurmountable barrier in my path, pushing that dream to the side for years. Fortunately, the idea didn't die completely, but remained a smoldering ember in my heart.

So, back to my rediscovery of Jack's work through that webinar I had found. At that time, I still hadn't written a book, but I had worn Canadian athlete, Jon Montgomery's Olympic Gold medal. And, while I wasn't prepared to climb a mountain or survive a dreaded disease as my big obstacle, my message emerged from my struggle with mental illness and the experience of overcoming it. In a moment of pure inspired action, I knew it was time to dust off that dream and make it a reality—I filled out the application form for the international Train the Trainer program. While my husband was supportive of me following this ambition, he wasn't prepared to finance it. I believed that somehow, I would find the money I needed. Within the week I received an unexpected cheque from my mom—an inheritance that she chose to share with her children, and the solution to my dilemma.

That path not only led me to learn about Success Principles, this was where I was first introduced to the concept of mindfulness and contemplation, through my work with Jack. As with any new thing, I struggled with learning how to do it and toiled at relaxing into a slowing of the mind. He mentioned a Vipassana retreat—ten days of silence—having a profound impact on his life and success.

I was fascinated! I wondered, *why would anyone want to shut up for ten days? And what good could possibly come from that?* I'm a communicator by nature. Talking and connecting with people is one of my strengths. Who and what would I be without that gift?

During a break, the curiosity took over and I questioned Jack about the Vipassana retreat, totally butchering the pronunciation in the process. He graciously corrected me on the pronunciation—*Vi-pu-shin-ah*—and his description somehow made sitting in quiet contemplation for sixteen-hour days very appealing. At least something in me found it alluring enough to take my next step in mindfulness and contemplation.

Shortly after completing my training with Jack I headed for what I referred to as Shut the Fuck Up Camp.

The story that unfolds in the pages of this book is a glimpse into my search for happiness and fulfillment. Longing to be clear on who I was, what I wanted, and eager to learn what I could along the way, I set out on a meandering path of discovery, a path that would take me far outside my comfort zone, where our true, authentic self usually awaits. What I didn't acknowledge at the start was that it would be a long journey, eventually transforming my life, allowing me to show up differently in the world. The expectation was that it would be loud, boisterous and filled with adventure.

Imagine my surprise when the answers came in the silence.

Since you've picked up this book, I'm guessing that, like me, you're on a quest of your own, seeking to discover what's missing from your life. Perhaps you once dreamed of doing, having, or being something else, and set that dream aside somewhere along the way. Perhaps, you've got some great things going on in your life and feel guilty about the sadness, resentment, or apathy that sometimes surfaces in your heart. Maybe you already know what's missing and simply need some direction on how to get it back.

Regardless of where you are in your journey and the obstacles in your path, this book will help you *Reignite Your Spark!*

Each chapter in this book follows my experience of a single day at "Shut Up Camp". I share my experiences exploring my external surroundings at the retreat, as well as my discoveries navigating my internal landscape - my mind, both conscious and subconscious, my heart and my soul.

Through my learning from the masters at this amazing, life-altering silent retreat, and through my stories, memories, observations and discoveries, you'll find that you too, can experience profound personal transformation, without having to shut up for ten days (though if the idea appeals to you, I highly recommend it).

At the end of each chapter, I've summed up the **Simple Steps to Reignite Your Spark**, which follow these five basic philosophies:

S - Stir Your Soul
P - Power Up Your Potential
A - Activate Your Awareness
R - Rock Your Resilience
K - Kick Ass With Intentional Action

Stir Your Soul steps will reawaken the authentic YOU, the core of your being and who you really are deep down inside. These steps will reacquaint you with your true self, that you are naturally, beneath all doubts and fears. At your center, you're an extraordinary, loving, and whole person, deserving of everything you ever truly wanted in life. Awaken that authentic you with these simple *Stir Your Soul* steps.

Power Up Your Potential steps will provide you with some great tips for boosting your results in whatever you're wanting to achieve. With a shift in perspective, these seemingly small adjustments will make all the difference in your life. The steps validate that there is more to you than you've been experiencing and that it's completely within your power to bring about a transformation. To "up level" your life and your results. Acknowledge that you're more than what you've allowed yourself to be with these simple *Power Up Your Potential* steps.

Activate Your Awareness steps keep you centered, focused and in the moment. The benefits of being aware in the present moment are numerous. You'll avoid fretting over past events which can't be changed, and you'll worry far less about possible future events which may or may not ever occur. Every moment you spend fully alive, alert and present to what's happening right now, is a moment without worry or regret. Give yourself this gift as often as possible with these simple *Activate Your Awareness* steps.

Rock Your Resilience steps gently guide you through letting go of past hurt and pain. For the best version of you to shine through and be Reignited, recognize that pain, regret, shame and suffering are NOT who you truly are, but rather are lessons and opportunities on the path of becoming who you truly are. And, they are obstacles that can be overcome with a little know-how. Break free from long-term suffering and disempowering emotion with these *Rock Your Resilience* steps.

Kick Ass With Intentional Action steps are the loving nudge you'll need to take the learning from this book and use it to transform your life. Knowledge is only a small part of any transformational journey. Application of knowledge is where real, lasting change occurs. Yet there is no rule saying that all actions have to be huge. You'll see that small actions, taken on a regular basis, will create big results in your life. *Kick Ass With Intentional Action* and see how the little things, consistently applied, can transform your life.

I'm so happy that you've chosen to Reignite Your Spark!

By coming with me on my journey into the silence, you'll rediscover your own brilliance, your own strengths, your own true gifts. You'll discover the source of your own power and learn how to employ it in your pursuit of a life you've only dreamed of thus far.

Day One

"Fear is at the root of so many of the barriers that women face. Fear of not being liked. Fear of making the wrong choice… And the holy trinity of fear: the fear of being a bad mother/wife/daughter."

Sheryl Sandberg, COO Facebook

"I felt powerful. I was choosing this adventure for me."

Day 1

Reignite Your Power

The severe winter storm warnings had started twenty-four hours earlier, and the weathermen were not exaggerating when they said severe. The snow was gusting horizontally. Visibility hadn't been too bad in Calgary, but as I travelled east toward the open Alberta prairies the fresh fallen powder was being whipped into a frenzy. I was relieved that I had only a short way to travel to my destination. I could barely make out the back end of two vehicles twenty feet in front of me as we crawled along. Heavy snowfall of up to 30 cm and blustery winds of 80 km per hour made for very poor driving conditions and people had been advised not to travel if it wasn't necessary. But this was necessary.

A ten-day silent meditation retreat was my destination. To shut out the chaos of a busy life was something I had longed for, and the idea of being surrounded by silence very much appealed to me. At one point, when I had three children under the age of three, I often fantasized about being stranded on a deserted island where no one needed anything from me. And now a decade or so later, I was getting that opportunity—at least metaphorically. The winter scene outside was far from a tropical island; however, it was giving me the timeout from my life that I really needed—and had for some time. I hoped the silence would give me a chance to focus on some of my questions about what I wanted in my life and what was stopping me from getting it—a quest that I had been on for a few years.

However, the whole idea of not talking or interacting with others had me on edge. Just thinking about it, I became aware of tightness in my chest. I was a talkative person by nature, and people who knew me were surprised that I would take on such a challenge. In fact, when I shared my plans with my friend Hal, he started to laugh so hard he cried, then doubled over with the thought of me restraining myself from the joys of chatting.

"You—not talking—for ten days?" He gasped between chuckles.

"Yeah, what's so funny about that?" I asked indignantly.

"Well, the fact that I don't think I've ever seen you be silent!" he retorted with amusement.

His response was by far the most dramatic. Most people had a momentary look of surprise, which they tried to hide because they were trying to be polite. Others gaped openly at me. There were many questions about my motives, and then people would start talking about their own ability to complete the task or why they wouldn't want to do it.

I had announced my plans to my family during a rare evening when we weren't running to extracurricular activities. Sitting together at the dinner table, I waited until everyone dished up their food, then opened the conversation by announcing that I had applied to participate in a ten day silent meditation retreat. Stewart, my husband, didn't say anything. Later that night he graciously agreed to hold down the fort while I was away, but in those first moments he sat quietly, listening to the kids—they had lots to say. My twelve-year-old daughter Shaelyn widened her big blue eyes and questioned, "But Mom, can't you die if you don't talk for ten days?"

Quickly, our dramatic fifteen-year-old daughter Sianna, jumped in to exclaim, "I know I would die if I couldn't talk. Are you allowed to cry? Cause I'd be over in the corner, curled up in a ball crying my eyes out until they let me talk."

I chuckled and assured Sianna that I expected to do some crying.

"Is this something Jack told you to do?" Rylee, our twelve-year-old son, asked. Barely pausing, he continued, "Because if it is, I think you should do it because you seem so much happier when you do the things that Jack tells you to do." He was referring to my mentor, Jack Canfield, one of the top human potential leaders in the world. I had just completed a year long Train the Trainer program where I honed my skills to teach success principles and habits. While he didn't tell me to do it, his mention of Vipassana meditation and the impact it had on his life, intrigued me.

So here I was driving through a terrible blizzard to get to the retreat, which I had started to refer to as "quiet camp." As I drove along the range road, there was a break in the weather long enough to see I was in a sub-division with huge, beautiful homes. When I pulled up to the address that I had been given, I was shocked to see another one of those magnificent houses. The sprawling, two-story, grey brick building appeared to be more like a castle, minus the spiraling towers. Slowly driving through the black wrought iron gates into the large curved driveway, I saw others unloading their vehicles and figured it must be the right place. I parked in front of one of the double car garages and proceeded into the grand entrance.

I had been expecting a rustic camp-like atmosphere with a main building and additional dormitory area for sleeping. I couldn't have been more wrong. I stepped out of the wind that cut right through my clothes and into the warmth of a beautiful foyer. Standing on the cream, marble tile, I marveled at the ornate table in front of me, adorned with a three-foot artificial Bonsai tree. I looked up at the twenty-foot ceilings and admired an incredible crystal chandelier. I felt like I was entering a five-star resort.

As I walked around the corner, the assistant teacher, Sharon, immediately met me. With her caring brown eyes and inviting smile, I felt an immediate maternal vibe from her. I estimated her to be in her mid-fifties and had the look of someone I could trust.

When I introduced myself her response was, "Oh, you're the one with the sleep machine." Before my arrival I had inquired by email whether my living quarters would have a power outlet because I required a CPAP machine as treatment for sleep apnea. The email response had questioned the noise level of the machine since I would be in shared accommodation with little room between beds. Maybe this was where I got the picture in my head of army barrack-style arrangements.

At any rate, I had replied to assure them that the machine was much quieter than the snoring and choking noises from me if I was unable to use the apparatus. Sharon and another staff member escorted me to a side room for a "sound test." *This really is quiet camp.* The machine passed the test, but Sharon decided it was best for me to be in a double rather than a room that four women would occupy.

I was elated to have more private sleeping quarters than expected. One perfect stranger felt more comfortable than being with a group of them. *I am glad I asked about the sleep machine!*

With the inspection completed, I was free to explore. From the magnificent entrance, the house got more spectacular as I moved further into it. To the right of the front door was a sitting area where the lofty ceilings continued, but I couldn't see much of it since temporary folding screens blocked the entrance. I found out later that it served as the eating area for the men.

In the center of the house, a grand staircase, five feet wide, rose to the second floor. A railing skirted the perimeter of an opening to the basement, ending at two separate descents, one on the left and one on the right. Looking over the railing, I could hear water running like a fountain, but I wasn't able to see the source of the relaxing sound. The entire stairway had been draped with white sheets to ensure the segregation.

From the main floor, ten beige carpeted steps led to a landing then split in either direction. To the left was a small area that overlooked the men's makeshift dining hall. Turning left again was the master suite and bath that five women would share. I descended to the landing and ventured across, up the stairs and along the walkway that adorned the right side of the second floor. Three more bedrooms, each with their own bathroom, were accessible from there.

I momentarily stood looking over the oak railing outside my room. I had an amazing view of the main floor living space and gourmet kitchen with floor to ceiling windows facing the west. I was in awe of what I had seen so far and despite my inner turmoil about the silent introspection; I felt solace about my physical surroundings.

Walking into my sleeping quarters, I breathed a sigh of relief. I was grateful to be settling in to an inviting and large space. There was nothing rustic or uncomfortable about this setting. Looking straight ahead was the door to our own private bathroom and parallel to the right wall was a single cot. In the left corner, what appeared to be a large corner desk was covered with a white sheet. This was normally an office space that converted nicely into accommodations for two women. Along the left wall were two long and narrow windows covered by simple cream-colored panel drapes. Placed perpendicular under the window was the second cot, and my bed for the next ten sleeps. Sitting on the simple wooden structure, it felt sturdy and very well built. The two-inch thick foam was a far cry from my comfortable fourteen-inch pillow top mattress at home, but it would have to do. There was no bedding provided so I set about unpacking a flat sheet to cover the mattress and my sleeping bag. This seemed as close as I would get to roughing it. I felt a little like I was at summer camp.

I soon found out that two brothers, with the intentions of hosting Vipassana retreats, had built the house. Two times a year, the resident family packed their belongings and vacated for ten days at a time, so strangers could benefit from their generosity.

After setting up my space and storing my luggage under the cot, I used our private bathroom. Again, the richness of the fixtures did not go unnoticed. Granite countertops and heated tile flooring was more like my dream house than a meditation venue. There were only two things that made it feel like the communal living it was meant to be. One was the red pail of cleaning supplies, clearly marked AVW for Alberta Vipassana Women and the second was an accordion drying rack for us to hang our personal towels. This stand was in front of a door, so I moved it and peeked inside to what I thought would be a small linen closet. It was a closet all right. I had entered a full walk-in closet complete with clothes and some of the items from the office. I felt like I was intruding on someone else's private space, so I quickly closed the door and replaced the rack in front of it.

More people were starting to arrive, and I could hear the tentative voices mingle with the welcoming staff dialogue; waft up from the main sitting room. While the refuge of my room was preparing me for the quiet ahead, I was curious about who would be sharing this experience with me. I also realized it was time to hand in my contraband items. One of the more challenging aspects of the ten days was going to be not journaling or reading. I hadn't brought any of that into the house but had a few books and my journal safely away from me in the van. My items to relinquish included the keys to my vehicle, my iPod, and cell phone.

As I started down the stairs, I noticed a missed call from the college where I was doing contract work. Stopping to listen, the voicemail informed me they needed to hear back from me regarding bookings for the New Year. I replied with a quick email that I would be unavailable to discuss until after their deadline. The universe had intervened and given me the opportunity not to respond. I had been thinking for a while that it was time to break away from this type of work and focus more on creating my own training courses. I already felt like a load had been lifted off my mind. I smiled as I handed over my belongings. Goodbye, outside world. Hello, inside world. I noticed the tightness in my chest was gone. I felt more relaxed, like a sponge soaking up the whole experience.

A lady sitting beside me at the registration table had a nosebleed. She noticed me and said, "I think I'm having an emotional reaction to handing in my cell phone." I chuckled and told her briefly how rewarding it had been for me. We struck up a conversation and soon were sharing very personal stories about ourselves. It didn't take long to learn that we both had nursing backgrounds, although she was still working in the profession as a manager in critical care. She had blond, highlighted shoulder-length hair and appeared to be in her late thirties. Sadness in her brown eyes and hardness in her face illustrated the story she told of a nasty divorce, custody battle, and past hurts by her family. I also saw a strength and determination to heal wounds and find happiness to share with her teenage son. There was an immediate connection with Rochelle, and I felt like we had been friends for many years. In fact, another lady, who had come to relinquish her belongings, commented that it would be nice to come with a friend. She seemed surprised when we told her that we had just met.

It was ironic that I had come to the retreat to get to know myself and to tap into my subconscious mind and there I was seeking out someone else to share the experience.

Intellectually, I knew this retreat was something I wanted to do, and I took pride in my decision. That ego part of me was okay to do it on my own. But emotionally it was a different story. Focusing on myself made me feel exposed and vulnerable. *If I connect with someone, it will feel less scary.* The truth was, I was afraid. What would I find in the silence? Being alone in a room was different than looking inside myself, and that was what I was about to do. It hadn't been my pattern or practice to do this for most of my life—

either as a wife, mother, or nurse. I had been focused on others. The thought of giving myself a little bit of my own attention was more than a little uncomfortable.

Rochelle and I continued to visit and connect through dinner as we waited for shut up camp to begin. I was only partially aware of other conversations around me as I focused on getting to know my new-found friend. After eating, all participants were brought into the main living room for orientation and the official welcome to the Vipassana retreat. One of the assistants reviewed the basics about the house, how meal times would work, and the boundaries inside and outside the house. There were large white sheets hung around the massive stairway structure to ensure a distinct barrier between the male and female common areas. We were to maintain complete segregation between men and women except for in the meditation hall. Even during orientation, the men sat in rows on the left side of the room and the women occupied the right side. Each group had separate entrances to the hall and exits to the outside of the house. I never really found out the reason for the split, and I assumed it was to serve as less of a distraction. It was easy to see how the needs of this type of retreat were kept in mind while they designed the house. The simple use of folding screens and bed sheets were all that was required to transform a home into a meditation center.

There seemed to be an electric charge in the air as we drew closer to the start of the course. Or maybe that was just what I was aware of in myself. I was confident that I would be able to last ten days without speaking. However, not speaking was only part of it. There was to be no eye contact, no gestures, no touching, and no acknowledgement of the people sharing the experience, which was referred to in the pre-course documentation as Noble Silence—the silence of the body, speech, and mind.

I knew that would present a challenge. Rochelle said, as we headed to the meditation hall, "Don't be offended if I quit speaking to you and totally ignore you." I laughed. I liked this gal. She had a great sense of humour. We made plans to go for coffee at the end of the retreat and then the silence began.

The ladies' entrance for the meditation hall was through a back mudroom into a double garage on the right side of the house then down a back staircase to the cozy dark basement. It was the perfect home theatre. Hanging on the front wall were two small TV screens, one in front of the men's side of the hall and one in front of the women's side. A square bench at the front about two feet high was the perch for the assistant teacher. On either side of her were a stereo and a shelf for the clock and some of her papers. Within the room there were 20 three-foot square meditation mats. A strip of paper with our names had been placed beside our assigned place on the floor.

My mat was in the front of the room to the right of the assistant teacher's mat. We quietly began to prepare our spaces on the floor, by arranging our meditation cushions and blankets, or wraps. I noticed most pillows were quite small and ranged in shapes, some rectangular and others circular. No two spots were created alike. At the top of the stairs there was a collection of foam blocks, pillows and foam wedges like those used in physiotherapy. Anyone who did not have a meditation cushion was free to choose from this pile to make sitting on the floor in one position for many hours as comfortable as possible.

My perch for the next ten days was not your typical meditation pad. Not wanting to purchase something new in case this whole meditation thing didn't work out, I took a look at home. As others walked in with nothing bigger than a cushion for sitting, I walked in with a two-foot by six-foot body pillow.

For Valentine's Day, many years before, I made the pillow to add to my husband, Stewart's collection. When he was a broke university student, he slept on large pillows fashioning them into a bed.

While he appreciated my intentions, he declared the black fun-fur covered sack too soft to sleep on. It may have been inadequate for his tastes but doubled over it was the perfect size and degree of softness for the meditation position I would take, many hours a day for the next ten. I giggled a little as I realized I towered over the other participants. My primary objective at this point was to find ultimate comfort, and as I twisted myself into my version of a lotus position, I felt pretty good on my big black furry stack of comfort. The other participants must have seen amateur written all over me.

My comfort lasted less than five minutes. I repositioned my legs and stretched them out. I shifted my butt from side to side. *Where did all that comfort go?* My lower back ached—no, my whole back ached. I concluded that I was the only person in the room who was too out of shape—to sit.

Fortunately, we were free to adjust our positions as much as we wanted. I felt like a toddler in a hard church pew, squirming around while the minister gave the sermon at the front of the room. I really wanted to lean over and ask the person beside me, “Does your ass hurt as much as mine?” Right then I decided that’s why we had to be silent, so we couldn’t lament our aches and pains to each other. At least one person in the room was going to have to toughen up and I realized it was me.

The teachings of Vipassana were led by S.N. Goenka, a guru from Burma through recordings on CD and DVD. The room was a little bit cool and lights had been dimmed slightly so there was an inviting hue. I jumped a little when the chanting first rang out of the speakers. A deep bass voice started to sing words that I did not understand. It seemed intrusive to the quiet at first and then became almost soothing. The chanting was followed by welcome and instruction. Goenka had a slow and deliberate way of speaking, and his accent was pleasing to listen to. The way he pronounced certain words made me smile.

As he spoke of what to expect and eloquently explained how we would be learning a simple and practical way to achieve real peace, harmony, and happiness, I knew that I had come to the right place. This is what I had been searching for. For a little over a year prior to this course, I had been exposed to the concept of meditation and how valuable it was in terms of getting in touch with our higher self, to find peace and calm in the chaotic world. When I was first introduced to meditation, my belief was that highly spiritual monks in white robes practiced it—generally on mountains. They became recluses to study the art and dedicate their life to it. During my training with Jack Canfield, I had learned that it had become more mainstream and some of the most successful people in the world identified meditation as a key success tool. Before attending this retreat, I had listened to guided audio sessions, always feeling like I wasn't quite getting it. When I heard about the Vipassana retreat, it sounded like Meditation University to me. Completely immersing myself in it for ten days and being instructed methodically was my style of learning.

Eagerness to listen to the teachings helped take some of the attention off of my aches and numbness. Goenka explained that hard work was necessary and that we would need to be diligent in following the teachings as they were given to us. The first step of the training was sîla or morality. We were asked to undertake five precepts: to abstain from killing any being, stealing, speaking falsely, sexual activity, and the use of all intoxicants. At first, I was confident in my ability to abide by these rules of morality.

I'm not in the practice of killing beings; however, I realized they were also referring to our food sources.

Eating a vegetarian menu was far different from anything I had experienced before. I grew up on a ranch in Alberta and we liked our meat. I was interested to see what the food would be like. I thought the precept of not killing any being was easy, but that night as I walked out of the hall I noticed a large spider on the floor and had to resist my natural instinct to squish it with my foot. I simply paused and walked around it.

As our guru laid out the ground rules, he confirmed Vipassana was not something that everyone was ready or able to do. He stressed that it would be a challenge. When I was researching the practice of Vipassana, I read a blog from a man who left after three days saying that he realized he had an aversion to rules and authority. My sister-in-law, Zina, also told me she heard by the third and fourth day people would leave. When I mentioned this to some of the other participants, a young woman named Renae explained she had taken the course three times before and only knew of one person leaving. I guess only time would tell. I was determined. I was up for the challenge and would endure whatever it took.

Once we agreed to *sîla,* we were able to move on to the second step of training our minds to be more concentrated and stable. Goenka gave the metaphor of trying to tame a wild elephant. Our stampeding, thrashing thoughts create havoc and chaos in our environment, but once the beast was quiet and trained it was very powerful. We were asked to request as a group, to be taught the Anapana meditation technique. As I said the words out loud and absorbed the voices of the others, I felt powerful. I was choosing this adventure for *me.*

We were instructed to keep our attention on the ever-changing flow of breath, being aware as it entered and left the nostrils. We were not to change or regulate our breathing. We were merely to notice it as it was. Keeping focus on a small triangle—the bridge of my nose at the top and my upper lip as the base—was not easy. Neither was staying aware of my breathing. *In, out, in, out, Ooh I have an itch on my eye. Concentrate. In, out, in… hmm feeling a little congested.* I shift my position to see if I can focus for longer than a nanosecond. *Start again.* Even as I wrote this, a smile came to my face as I heard Goenka say at the beginning of many of the sittings, "Staaart Agaaain, Staaart Agaaain, Staaart with a determined and diligent mind." The breathing was not to be forced, but we were instructed that if the mind was agitated or wandered easily we should breathe slightly harder to improve our ability to increase awareness. At first, I sounded like a heavy breather on a prank phone call since my mind wandered easily and I was emphasizing my breath. When the chant started, signaling the end of the meditation hour, I was relieved. *All of this breathing takes a lot of effort!* We were given a short break before returning to the hall for the evening lesson, or discourse as it was called.

"The first day is over and you have nine more to go." *When you put it that way it sounds like a huge hurdle to get over.* Goenka said these talks were not for intellectual entertainment but for us to understand the technique and how we were to work. *So much for settling in with a bowl of popcorn.* Emphasis was put on the specialty of *Anapana*. This was not a breathing exercise to regulate or control our breath. The technique was to observe the reality of the breath as it was, not as we would like it to be. I smiled when he said, "The first day is a difficult day. The students complain of back pains or leg pains, of this discomfort or that discomfort." *Holy cow! It's like he is in my head. Good to know I'm not the only one experiencing this.*

Goenka continued on to say that we had become prisoners of our own mind and body. The habit pattern of life was that if we do something we are unaccustomed to, our mind and body revolt. Other meditation techniques use visualizations or mantras and he agreed that concentration of the mind was easier that way. "The final goal of Vipassana is to purify the mind." *Great, I always joke that my mind is in the gutter. Better keep listening.* We are taught to relax at the surface level but don't realize the root of our problems are the negativities at the deepest part of our mind. *I understand that our negative thoughts and limiting beliefs are part of our subconscious mind, but I don't get how awareness on our breathing will help clear those.* Goenka continued, saying that as we explored our awareness, we would start with gross realities and continue to more subtle realities and sensations. *Huh?* As we focused on the sensations on our bodies, we would realize the truth pertaining to our mind and matter. We started with the breath only. As we progressed we would explore the truth about our bodies. *I took anatomy and physiology in university. What truth didn't I learn?* Again, as if he was in my head, he answered that what we learn about in science is intellectual knowledge.

Goenka explained that what we know about our mind and bodies at an experiential level is very little. Buddha, or the enlightened one, found the tool to experience what's happening within the framework of the body—the breath. The breath works like a bridge, so we can move from the known field of the physical structure to the unknown field. Then he stressed that we should only accept these teachings when we experienced them, not because of what he told us.

I am trying so hard to take all of this in. I hope I can actually get to the point where I experience this. I have spent the last thirty years of my life staying in my head and pushing feelings, and sensations away.

"Nobody told you to observe the mind, but unintentionally you noticed the mind," he said. *I noticed the mind—wandering aimlessly.* He described the two places for the mind to wander, past memories or thoughts of the future. According to the teachings, our mind does not want to live in the present, so it becomes agitated. When we have pleasant memories, we enjoy that sensation and want to enjoy it again, so our subconscious mind develops a craving or clinging. Similarly, with an unpleasant memory, we create an aversion or hatred. While the conscious level of the mind stays busy with our external environment and distraction, we are unaware that deep in our subconscious we are creating misery bouncing between craving and aversion. This negativity and constant reaction happens at the deepest level.

Goenka used the metaphor of Vipassana being a deep surgical operation of our own minds. When we cut open the wound, the pus starts coming up on the surface, and it is for our own good, but the whole process is very difficult. He described that we would experience pain and discomfort, but we must not run away. There would be no outside surgeon and no anesthesia. He equated the rules and schedule of the course to a hospital. *Now he is speaking my language, I can totally relate to the hospital and surgical metaphor.*

Goenka finished the evening discourse on a positive note telling us that by exploring the truth about our mind and body we would find inner peace, harmony and happiness. *Excellent! That is what I'm here for!*

At the end of the session some of the "old students" chanted a response. This was how returning students were referred to and they had additional precepts to follow. I was curious about it the first time but had too many other things running through my mind to question it. He explained that he concluded sessions with "*Bhavatu sabba mangalan,* which translates to: "May all beings be happy!" The response was "Sadhu, sadhu, sadhu," meaning "Well said, well done; we agree, we share this wish." I thought this was a nice sentiment and chose to respond, even though it wasn't a requirement.

By 9:00 p.m. we were released from the meditation hall. Some stayed behind to ask questions of the assistant teacher. My mind was whirling at a frenetic pace, but I wasn't able to formulate any real questions. I retreated to my room for some much-needed sleep. The morning gong was scheduled to go off at four a.m. Prior to the silence; my roommate, Veronica and I had discussed logistics of sharing a bathroom. She preferred to bathe in the evenings, and I was a morning shower girl so that arrangement was ideal. I quickly brushed my teeth, washed my face, and as I stood looking in the mirror, I realized that sleep was not likely to come quickly. My thoughts were racing and bouncing around in my head.

As I lay down I attempted Anapana. I focused on observing the rise and fall of my breathing to see if I could relax and unwind. Attention to the triangle on my face came easy as my sleep apnea mask provided the perfect perimeter. The habit pattern of the mind, as I had learned tonight, was to be busy and chaotic. The technique was to quiet the mind, have awareness of sensations on my body, tap in to the subconscious, and find happiness. I knew the quietening of the mind was going to take some time, and it would certainly not be mastered that night.

I tossed. I turned. I reviewed the activities of the day. I looked at the clock. I changed positions again. At midnight I got up to the bathroom and thought, *Okay, four hours of sleep.*

The last time I looked at the clock it said 2:30. I drifted off to sleep, filled with anxiety about how I would cope with the rigors of sitting quietly for long periods of time and stay awake to meditate later that day.

Simple Steps to Reignite Your Power

Stir Your Soul | What seemingly outrageous idea has been brewing at the back of your mind or deep within your heart? Consider the possibility that NOW could be the time for you to turn that dream into a reality.

Power Up Your Potential | Acknowledge your own power. Recognize that you create your own misery through mental and emotional chaos, bouncing between a craving for pleasure and an aversion to pain. Think of your mind as a wild elephant which can be tamed.

Activate Your Awareness | Initially, observe your life as it is, not as you would like it to be. Before your Spark can be Reignited, get comfortable with the truth of where you are right now. Only by recognizing the truth can you move toward something better.

Rock Your Resilience | Begin with a determined and diligent mind. When you embark on a journey outside of your comfort zone, life may throw obstacles in your path. I'm not advocating putting yourself in danger, but don't allow yourself to be easily swayed from achieving what you desire.

Kick Ass With Intentional Action | Take one little step toward doing something that you've dreamed of doing. Make a phone call, do some research on the Internet, pick up a book about someone who has done what you'd like to do.

Day Two

"Others inspire us, information feeds us, practice improves our performance, but we need quiet time to figure things out."

Ester Schaler Buchholz, The Call of Solitude: Alonetime in a World of Attachment

"It took more courage and strength to show my emotions than it would have to act like I had it all together."

Day 2

Reignite Your Strength

I woke and looked at the clock. 3:55 a.m. I knew the gong would sound in five minutes over the speaker system. Normally, I would close my eyes and strive for a few more moments of precious sleep, but I felt alert and eager to get started. When the bell did ring, I waited for Veronica to use the washroom and then showered and dressed. The second chime rang at 4:20, and I could hear people leave their rooms for the meditation hall. I was surprised at how refreshed I felt, considering I had little more than two hours of solid sleep. I was eager to get started in my practice.

Taking my time to get into position and ensure that I was comfortable, I noticed there were only about ten people in the hall. The early morning meditation could be done in the hall or in "your place," meaning your room. I mentally patted myself on the back for being so diligent and getting up when I hadn't slept well. It would have been easy to stay in bed and sleep. Closing my eyes, I took a deep breath and focused my attention on the triangle on my face. My breathing was natural and maybe a little shallow, but the idea was not to change it, just be aware. I lasted about thirty seconds before the first mind drift started.

Someone sneezed. Someone came into the room. I was acutely aware of everything going on around me. It wasn't much but it served as a great distraction to the task at hand. I went back and forth between fleeting moments of great awareness on my breathing and completely random thoughts. The alertness I felt upon awakening was gone. Several times I jumped, realizing I had drifted off to sleep. *Where was all this relaxed state last night when I was trying to sleep?*

Eventually, thinking it must be time for breakfast I left the meditation hall. The house was quiet. I returned to my room and realized only thirty-five minutes had passed. My internal clock was way out of whack. I thought of Stewart, with his finely tuned inner chronometer. He was able to accurately state the time of day within several minutes, not using a timepiece. Not me—I relied heavily on my watch but had forgotten it at home. Perhaps the universe had intervened on my behalf, and I wasn't meant to have it. I did however, have a travel alarm clock, which gave me some solace.

So, I have an hour and a half before the breakfast gong rings. I hesitated only a fraction of a second before climbing into bed. I lied to myself and said that I would meditate "in my place" knowing full well I would quickly fall asleep. As I drifted off, I wondered if I had broken the sîla of abstaining from wrong speech—I never actually spoke the lie out loud.

The breakfast bell woke me from a sound sleep. I splashed cold water on my face wanting to give the impression that I had been awake and meditating for hours. *Wait a minute; I'm an adult. Why am I so worried about what others think? This is my experience and if I want to sleep that's my decision. Where is this guilt coming from? Isn't this supposed to be about me?*

I ventured off to breakfast, attempting to quiet the chatter inside of me.

This was our first meal with no talking. Everyone was a bit tentative as they approached the buffet set up on the kitchen island. It was as though we were all learning how to occupy the space and move within it. Normally, I would be making small talk as I moved through the line, commenting on the food or asking how everyone's morning meditation (or sleep) was. Instead, I observed the food.

A steaming pot of thick, stick-to-your-ribs oatmeal was the main entree. I recognized the stewed prunes from my days of working on the geriatric floor in the hospital. I passed—didn't need those just yet. There was a large bowl of apples, oranges, pears, and bananas, and on the side counter a toaster and good selection of breads. Suspiciously absent was a coffee pot. A large assortment of herbal teas and almond milk was available and tucked behind those I found some instant coffee—decaffeinated! *So much for savouring my morning cup of java. The caffeine would have really helped me stay awake during meditation.*

I didn't feel the need to linger over a second cup of coffee. There was no stimulating conversation to keep me there, so I decided to climb onto the large cream-colored sectional that had been pushed into the corner. I liked being in the common area, looking out and watching as the sky brightened in preparation for sunrise. I couldn't remember the last time I was awake to watch the start of the day.

I reflected on what mornings were like at home. Catch the last possible moments of slumber, wake to an intrusive alarm, and then stumble out of bed to get the kids up for school. Sometimes I'd climb back in bed. Back to rouse the kids again, then stagger in to the shower to try and wake up.

I liked the quiet here. The calm was soothing. I continued to look out the window, and before long I was running through my to-do list in my head. I was successfully avoiding looking inside, one more time.

It was hard to remember which random and obscure things ran through my head on which day. The first days were really very practical things like mentally reorganizing my cupboards, thinking about purging the clutter from my basement, and prioritizing all the things I needed to do for my fledgling business. I had a list of things to do. I found it much easier to let my mind wander on those than stay focused on the task of observing breath.

We had three one-hour sessions per day that were mandatory group sits. Everyone was required to meditate in the hall. At other times we took direction about where to meditate from the assistant teacher. The morning sit started at 8 a.m. Participants filtered in and settled in their spots. I kept my eyes down so I wasn't tempted to acknowledge them. The male and female managers were the last to arrive through their respective entrances, and I saw them as the guardians of the flock. Once everyone was settled, Sharon arrived and walked almost silently through the mats. As I closed my eyes, she clicked on the recording and the room was once again filled with chanting.

The pain in my back started immediately. My legs and the rest of my body were more malleable to the position than the night before, but I needed a bit of support for my back that was weakened from past injuries. Shifting positions was a short-term solution. I thought of the participant who had one of those stadium seats. Two pieces of padding held together by a strap that shaped it into a mini-chair. Those would be handy to have in the motorhome for taking to the beach. *Oh yeah right… breathe. Notice the breathing, Carla. Stop letting your mind wander. Get this right!* I planned to check for pieces of foam to help support my back. The good news was that I did notice that the stretches of focus on my breathing grew longer before once again letting the wild elephant come crashing through my mind.

Most of the teaching was done in the evening discourse, but during daily sits the learning was reinforced with Goenka's gentle reminders. After the chant, the teacher called four student names to sit in front of her. When I heard my name, I felt like I was being called to the principal's office and I didn't know why. Sharon looked at me and asked, "Were you able to feel the sensation of your breath in the small focus area?" I told her "yes." She smiled warmly and moved on to my roommate who responded, "Yes, I feel sensations through the whole body like electricity."

Great, I can barely hold my focus on breathing and she is feeling sensations all through her body. I wish I felt sensations through my whole body. I was surprised when Sharon told her that was great, but not what we were supposed to be doing. *Being a high achiever and trying to move ahead of the class is not the approach to take. One step at a time, I'm doing fine.* The last person in our quad said, "I'm having a hard time staying awake and on task." *She's so honest. I wish I had admitted that I was having the same struggles. Why didn't I?* After responding with gentle reassurance and compassion Sharon said, "Let's meditate together for some time." I counted the time in my head as I was really looking forward to getting back to my spot. These mats at the front were a far cry from my enormous cozy cushion.

My personal level of comfort seemed to be a significant trend in the first days. I realized I was being stretched on many levels. First, twisting myself into a position on the floor for long periods of time. Next, being aware of the sensations that were coming up in this new practice. Most importantly was the mental issue of looking inside myself. I was feeling more strongly the emotional discomfort. Reflecting on Goenka's words from the night before I realized that I had a long-standing aversion to dealing with emotions—an aversion that went back over thirty years.

On graduation night, three decades prior, my fourteen-year old brother, Dale was killed in a car accident. Our world came to a screeching halt. I remember walking around as though I was watching a movie of someone else's life. I became an unattached observer. I watched my parents as they tried to be strong for their children. I watched as they broke down and cried, and then I watched as they very quickly brought themselves under control. Sitting in the hard, wooden pew at the church, filled with hundreds of people from our small town, I thought, *"You have to be strong. Don't cry."* I was afraid. Afraid that if I started to cry and really felt the emotion, I wouldn't be able to stop. So, I didn't show the outside world what I felt inside and eventually my habit was to dismiss my own feelings. I shoved them in a box.

It was time to open that box. To heal. To connect to the deep happiness and joy that I had experienced as a child. I hoped that this retreat would help me do that.

Wandering into the dining area I migrated toward the bulletin board with the daily agenda. My intention was to kill time by rereading the same information I had already reviewed several times. I noticed a signup sheet to meet with the teacher during our lunch break.

Suddenly, I was overwhelmed with the thought that I needed to meet with her to ask to be moved against the wall. I'm not sure why this hadn't occurred to me before. It was as though someone just dropped the idea into my head. My default behaviour was to accept the situation and not ask to make concessions even in the interest of comfort.

After lunch I waited to be summoned by Melanie, the women's manager. No words were spoken, but we did make eye contact and she nodded at me. It felt a little clandestine. I followed her to the basement where Sharon waited on her seat, looking very serious. Seated before her, I couldn't help thinking it was a bit like having an audience with the queen. The lights were dimmed, and it felt somber. When I first started to speak my voice was a hoarse whisper. I cleared my throat and said, "I was wondering if I could be moved to sit against the wall, so I have support for my back?" *Why do I feel uneasy making a simple request? It's not like I'm asking for much.*

Sharon gave me a reassuring smile and asked if I had a problem. *Do I need a valid reason?* I told her that I had a back injury from falling off a horse many years ago and my back was weak. She replied, "Of course we can move you, but right now everyone feels like they fell off a horse as they are trying to adjust. You didn't have that on your intake form."

I retorted, "But I really did fall off a horse, I just didn't think that was relevant until I started to do this." *Again, with that smile.* In the end, my request was easily granted and the two of them started to reconfigure the space. I was pleased with myself for speaking up and looking after my needs.

It was easy to spot my new space when I entered the hall after my conversation with Sharon. My mat and cushions had been nicely arranged against the back wall. As I settled into my place for the one-hour group sit, the support of the wall was comforting. Day two my physical discomfort was mostly taken care of. I have to admit I was proud of myself for putting my needs first—another thing that had not been a part of my personal habits and practices.

I grew up in a traditional home on the farm. My dad worked outside, and the house and the children were mom's domains. She had trained as a certified nurse aide but did not have a job outside of the home at any time that we were growing up. My mom dedicated her life to caring for us. I watched as she devoted her time to pack us lunches, have a hot meal on the table, care for our clothes and drive us to endless volleyball, hockey, or 4-H activities.

With her modeling the expected behaviour of a wife and mother, I assumed that I was to behave the same. What I didn't know was that I had a choice. And if I had given it any thought, I wouldn't have chosen her path.

I can remember the day clearly when this started to become obvious to me.

The sun was shining on my face. A breeze kept the air moving so it was hot, but not hot enough to make you sweat—just comfortable. I was stretched out on the recliner, looking out from the deck over my nicely landscaped yard. The log cabin playhouse Stewart had designed and built was the backdrop for our three kids as they ran under the sprinkler.

They giggled and screamed as the cold water drenched their warm skin. I could hear the river outside the gate through the tall poplar trees as it flowed lazily along. I had nowhere to be but right where I was.

When I reflected on that scene, I realized I was unaware of that tranquility, beauty, laughter, or love that surrounded me. As I looked on that day, I felt nothing. Well, that's not completely true—I felt numb and empty. The anti-depressant medication I was taking kept me from experiencing the lows and the sadness, but it also kept me from experiencing the joys in my life.

That day, I had a moment of clarity, where I stopped long enough to take a look at what was happening and listened to something deep inside me that said, "There is a better way." That day, I decided to take back my life. I made a choice to go off the medication.

The truth is I had been giving away my personal power for years.

When I had the opportunity to make choices I focused on what others thought. I abandoned myself; choosing actions that I thought would please others around me. I was so desperate to be liked and loved that I would do what I thought I should do rather than what I wanted. Come to think of it I didn't stop and figure out what I wanted at all. And I knew I wasn't alone in that.

I was coming back from Jack Canfield's Breakthrough to Success (BTS) and his "decide what you want" principle had a profound impact on me. At the airport restaurant, I stood looking at the menu. I was taking the time to look at all the options, trying to decide what I wanted to eat, not what should I eat, but what I felt like eating. I listened to what my body was telling me. I made a choice in favour of me. As I was standing there a man came up behind me, and I said, "Go ahead if you know what you want. I'm still trying to decide." He looked me in the eye and said, "Honey, if I knew what I wanted, my life wouldn't be such a mess. That's the story of my life. I don't know what I want." He shrugged his shoulders and walked away.

Most of us have been conditioned by our families, our bosses, and society in general to ignore our desires. Or perhaps even worse, we have conditioned ourselves to put our wants and needs on hold to care for others, and we simply let others tell us what we want. Slowly, I began practicing making choices in favor of myself, including the one that lead me to this meditation retreat.

Following the group sit, we were free to meditate in the place of our choosing. I decided to stay in the hall. One of the things Sharon said during our discussion that afternoon really resonated with me. I had admitted to the struggles of unplanned micro sleeps and a dangerously wandering mind. She suggested meditating in the hall, as there was an energy that existed when many people were present. When I stopped to think about it, I did feel like I had an easier time focusing during times in the hall as opposed to in my room. Besides, it was easier to stay awake in a sitting position than supine on my bed. It didn't hurt to take her advice. It also didn't hurt to draw energy or strength from those around me when I needed it.

That was something new I was learning to do in my life. Letting go of the need to be fiercely independent. I was learning to ask for what I wanted, and also allowing others to help me. And sometimes this felt really scary. Leaning on someone else made me feel vulnerable and exposed. And it was apparently something I needed to practice, as circumstances arose in my life that made it imperative to learn this lesson.

In June of 2013, steady rainfall for four days swelled the river behind our house to dangerously high levels. I witnessed my neighbour, Randy, pacing past our house to the river. It was the middle of the afternoon and unusual for him to be home from work, so I was on alert.

That evening I met my neighbour Jack and several others on the driveway. We discussed the reality that our sewers would likely back up and our basements would be flooded. Standing in the rain surrounded by people, I felt completely alone—particularly since Stewart was hiking Machu Pichu in Peru. When I asked what I should be doing, Randy helped me sandbag the basement drain. He also carried some of the valuables out of the basement for me. When we reconvened outside, Jack said he would be staying up to monitor his basement and would wake me if the sewer backed up. Before crawling into bed, I comforted the kids telling them, "We won't be evacuated. Worst case scenario is we have some flooding in the basement and that can be fixed." I was trying to comfort myself as much as the kids.

The doorbell woke me from a sound sleep around four in the morning. I glanced at the clock as I stumbled out of bed and threw on my robe. Once I reached the top of the stairs, the pounding on the door began. Half way down the stairs, I heard banging at the back door. The dog was going nuts in the laundry room. My chest tightened as the adrenaline surged through me. My hands were shaking, and I fumbled to get the deadbolt unlocked. Before I got the door open—I knew it wasn't Jack.

I stood face to face with a female police officer. Suddenly, the chaos of the dog barking wildly and the intensifying throttling at the back door felt like a bad dream. I was transfixed as she called on the radio to tell the officers standing at the back door that I was there with her. The pounding stopped. The dog did not. The officer informed me that we needed to prepare to evacuate. I must have said something, and she repeated that we did not need to leave yet—just prepare.

I would like to say that I jumped into action and was in total charge. I was dazed. My fifteen-year-old daughter, Sianna, took charge. I looked out the window thinking I would see everyone's lights on and activity in the houses, so I wouldn't feel like this was just happening to us. Nothing. Across the street the houses were dark. Sianna snapped me out of the stupor and said, "You pack your stuff and Rylee's, and I'll pack mine and Shaelyn's."

I quickly threw some clothes in suitcases and decided I needed to find out why nobody else was in emergency mode.

Peering out my front door I saw lights on in the three houses to the left of me. I walked two doors down to Clark and Tina's, and when the door opened, I saw the suitcases by the door. They appeared prepared and calm to me. I asked Clark, "Is this really happening?" His response was to take me onto their back deck. The river was raging just ten feet away. The trees that once provided a break in the view were gone, along with the riverbank. I burst into tears and said, "I have to be at work in a few hours." *That made a whole lot of sense. The safety of my home and family were in jeopardy, and I am worried about letting someone down at work.* "Carla, you are not going to work," Clark admonished. I felt silly that I needed somebody to tell me what should have been obvious. At the same time relief washed over me as I realized I wasn't alone. I had someone to support me.

As we stood together on the deck, I tried to sort my thoughts and control my emotions. I apologized for crying. He wrapped his arms around my shoulders and pulled me into a hug. My arms hung at my side, and I laid my face, wet from rain and tears against his chest. For just a moment, I let my guard down, let his embrace comfort, and make me feel safe. I cried harder. My long-held disposition of being strong, tough, and in control was crumbling quickly. The sound of the river rushing by snapped me back to the situation. Those few minutes of human compassion gave me the courage I needed. I took a deep breath and pulled away. It was time to get back home to finish packing. I felt a little better knowing that I wasn't in this alone. Sianna had a pile of suitcases and treasured items at the door. We continued to gather belongings. I left a voicemail for the coordinator at the college to apologize that I wouldn't be in to conduct training. My voice broke when I told her my husband was gone, so I was the only one here to deal with the emergency.

By six a.m. Clark's son, Charles, was knocking on the door to ask what we needed help carrying to the van. A paramedic told him they wanted us to evacuate to the emergency meeting point—we had fifteen minutes. I saw the emergency response team milling around in the cul de sac as we hurried to throw suitcases, photo albums, home movies, our dog Bandit's supplies, and everything we could into the van. This was the first time I had been grateful to be driving a mom mini-van! We were in such a rush we didn't realize until later that night that we put our clothes and toiletries underneath all of the memorabilia. Our urgent packing also resulted in Rylee wearing my socks for the next three days. Looking back, I was so charged with adrenaline I didn't take the time to stop, take a breath, recognizing that our lives were not in immediate danger. We were being asked to leave as a precaution. That was where the rational, in-charge personality of Stew would have come in handy.

In our neighbourhood, only families in the four houses backing directly on to the river had been asked to evacuate. Jack was packing up his wife, Nicolette, and baby Rachel. Her father was there to go with her while Jack stayed at the house. Richard and Kelly had called a friend to pick up their two-year-old twins. They refused to leave. Clark said he was only going because if something catastrophic did happen he wanted to be sure his cooperation was documented for insurance purposes. It never even occurred to me to decline. It never crossed my mind to say "no." I was doing what Clark was doing—he was my support. I was on autopilot. I was crying openly as the kids waited in the van and I stood with Clark, Jack, Randy, and some of the other neighbours who had gathered in the middle of the street. One of the neighbours who were not being asked to leave questioned what I was crying about. I couldn't formulate the words to answer. I cried harder and climbed into the driver's seat.

Driving away from the house with my kids, my dog, and a vanload of memorabilia, I felt nauseous. Not the nausea where

I might throw up, just a sick feeling in the pit of my stomach. I followed Clark and his family to the evacuation site. We checked in with the social worker that was sitting in the back of a cargo van. She questioned each person to determine names of family members and pets that were displaced. When she asked if we needed a place to stay, I told her we would be staying with my brother and sister in-law. I hadn't made these arrangements, but the words popped out of my mouth. So, I was capable of making some decisions on my own.

I received a social services emergency intake form. I used to sarcastically joke if someone called to report me as an unfit mother, I would get a respite from my motherly duties while they did the assessment. I said as much to Clark while we stood in the parking lot of the arena. I had regained some composure and was trying to inject humour into the situation. Clark smiled and let out a chuckle, but he was distracted. I'm not sure he even heard me. It was as though I could see the wheels turning in his head as he contemplated the next move.

Since there was no immediate threat and we had done our duty by registering, Clark told me he was going back home. The kids and I followed in the van. As we drove back onto our street, we noticed police tape in a big yellow X on the front door of our home. I knew from my days as an emergency response officer that meant that the house had been cleared and no one was staying there.

I stood on Jack's back deck with the men of the neighbourhood, watching the river. I was kind of glad Stew wasn't there because I got to hang with the guys instead of sitting inside with the women, drinking coffee, and caring for the children. Jack offered me a smoke. I said, "No, but I could use a shot of tequila." I was only half-kidding. He laughed and got a bottle and a glass for me. I had no idea what time it was, but it couldn't have been later than 10 a.m.

One of the best shots of tequila I have had in my life!

That was Tuesday. I made arrangements for the kids and I to stay with Stewart's brother, Shannon. The river had peaked by midday and we were safe enough to be in the house, but I chose not to sleep there. I refused to repeat the trauma of a visit from the police in the middle of the night. By Wednesday, things settled into a routine of watching and waiting. I dropped the kids to school and returned to the neighbourhood. Thursday was the day the waterworks started again. Not the rain. Me. The forecast was calling for 100 mm of rain. I walked with Lynne and Randy to see the rows of sandbagging that had been placed by volunteers the night before. The riverbank continued to erode at an alarming rate behind the houses. The mayor was called to the site. Suddenly, things were urgent, and I was crying—again.

Later that afternoon a mandatory evacuation was enforced for the whole subdivision so there was no more going back and forth. Most of the men and a few families refused to leave. Clark and Jack both told me to go. My priority was the kids. They assured me that they would look after the house. That was on Friday. The kids were in school, and it was only Bandit and I at my in-laws. I was frustrated to be separated from the group, to not know what was happening. I also disliked feeling helpless. Even though there was really nothing I could do, it was that sense of not being in control that had me troubled. When I look back though, letting go gave me relief. All I chose to do was nap and read with the dog curled safely in my lap. I let "the boys" handle the situation. Handle it they did. A 500-ton crane was brought in to place huge cement blocks in the river to stop the erosion and save the houses.

As I reflected on this event, the emotions rushed back and most of it was written with tears streaming down my face. Sianna asked what I was so upset about. That whole experience touched me deeply. At the time, I was embarrassed that I was crying because I associated it with being weak. For me it took more courage and strength to show my emotions than it would have been to act like I had it all together. I allowed myself to be vulnerable by showing that I was afraid. I also experienced basic human love, compassion, and support. That emotional connection with others was something I had held at arm's length for many years. I was holding the emotional connection with myself at bay as well.

And I was coming to terms with it at the retreat.

"Second day, slightly better than the first day." I smiled at the way Goenka spoke to us in the evening discourses. He used the analogy of a monkey swinging from branch to branch, and our minds jumping from thought to thought rapidly. I felt a shiver go up my spine when he said, "No one can harm us more than our own wild mind, and no one can help us more than our own trained, disciplined mind." *This is all about me.* I thought of the years I was treated for clinical depression. I had many visits to the doctor, the psychiatrist, and a psychologist. I had read numerous self-help books. I was looking for answers outside of myself when what I needed was to connect to the answers within me.

The irony was for years I felt my depression was a result of pushing my feelings away. I felt that I was stuck in my head and not paying attention to my heart. Now here I was being told that it was about training the mind in order to be in touch with sensations and feelings. The wild mind for me was listening to all of the outside sources, creating stories in my mind that amplified my limiting beliefs, my self-doubts, and my criticisms. Even before I attended this retreat, I had started a meditation practice. When I spent quiet time and focus on my thoughts, I gained clarity about who I was and what I wanted. The answers were coming from within rather than from the outside.

I always thought that Buddha was the name of a wise man. I did not realize that it means enlightened one—one who had tamed a wild mind.

Goenka informed us that everyone could become a Buddha but not in ten days. *The pressure is off. I don't have to master this technique in ten days! Great advice for me as a recovering perfectionist.*

I remember very clearly the day I made a conscious decision to be perfect. I had witnessed my parents go through the most gut-wrenching pain of their lives and doing the best they could, they picked up the pieces and carried on for us—the four remaining children. They sacrificed working through their own grief in an open and healing way so that they could help us get through. In the logic of a fourteen-year-old girl who had witnessed such anguish, I thought that if I was perfect, achieved awards, worked really hard and never did anything wrong in the eyes of my parents I could spare them any more pain. I hoped I could make them happy again.

I set standards that were impossible to keep. I believed that if I could live my life perfectly then I would be happy again, and so would everyone around me. I also hoped that I could keep pain away. That I wouldn't have to hurt ever again.

The words of Goenka popped back in to interrupt my thoughts. "When we experience impurities in our mind - anger, negativity, hatred, animosity, greed, ego, jealousy, fear - nature starts punishing us. When you generate these feelings you become agitated, so unhappy, so miserable. When you stop generating these thoughts then you are rewarded with peace and tranquility." I reflected on an exercise I had done at Breakthrough to Success where we were being muscle tested by a partner. We were asked to think of someone or something that really got under our skin. When I had that vision, my strength was significantly reduced. When I had positive loving thoughts, my arm was nearly unmovable.

Again, Goenka's next statement hit me with impact. "You are the first victim of your anger." He explained that when we give importance to the outside world we don't notice how we are being punished. He stated, "Heaven and Hell are within us." *Grandma Phyllis used to say something like that. I'll have to ask Dad—when I can talk again.*

My mind was overflowing but the discourse continued, and I tuned back in to concentrate on the teachings. I wanted to find out how all of this would be accomplished by focusing on our breathing.

It was explained that anyone who walks on the path to enlightenment would become a more noble and good-hearted person. *The challenge is to stop generating all of those negative beliefs and thoughts. He's right. This is going to be hard work. That's where the diligent and patient reminders come in. My mind is so full! Maybe the escape I was so desperate for all those years was an escape from my thoughts not my external environment. Will I really connect to my heart and who I am if I train my mind to be pure of the negativity?*

Goenka urged us to put our awareness on the present moment rather than dwelling on the past or worrying about the future. By focusing on our breath, we would sharpen our abilities to notice the constant sensations within our bodies. In the beginning we would experience what Goenka referred to as gross solidified intense sensations like pain, itching, or numbness. I was reassured that with practice we would be capable of noticing more subtle sensations. Our job was simply to observe what we felt in our bodies and not react to it. From moment to moment the reality would change and so would the sensation. *I change positions to alleviate the pain. Maybe I'll try observing it and wait for it to pass. Emotional pain could be resolved this way too. By noticing and allowing it to happen rather than suppress it maybe it will pass more quickly.*

As we mastered our mind, our guru told us we would reach the deepest part of our mind the unconscious. By doing this, we would purify the source of our misery. *This is what I'm here for. To tap in to the subconscious and clear out the negativity, the fear, the misery.* The process was to create no new cravings or aversions and the old *saṅkhāras*—reactions—would be brought to the surface. Once brought to the surface, we would observe them, and they would pass away. *This sounds amazing. Like house cleaning or purging clutter.*

"The opportunity is good for you here. Study the universal technique of Vipassana diligently, patiently, ardently and you will come out of your misery to enjoy real peace, real harmony, real happiness," Goenka says.

And with that the chanting finished the evening discourse. We had a small break to stretch our legs before returning to the hall for the final meditation of the night. I slowly walked upstairs, put my shoes on and stepped out the front door. The cold air stung my nostrils and my lungs as I took a deep inhale. I needed fresh air. My thoughts were racing, and I was so excited I could feel my heart beating. Another deep breath. *So much information to process. This is definitely the right place for me.*

A third deep breath and I rose to re-enter the house, making my way to the hall to finish for the night.

Simple Steps to Reignite Your Strength

Stir Your Soul | Consider what would happen if you expressed and released your emotions more—whether happy or sad, confident or fearful.

Power Up Your Potential | Allow others to help you. It takes courage and strength to be vulnerable with others, which leads to deeper human connections.

Activate Your Awareness | Become aware of how quickly you accept things as they are, rather than ask for something different. Small things, like being shown to a table at a restaurant when you'd rather sit at a booth.

Rock Your Resilience | When you stop generating feelings of anger, negativity, animosity, jealousy and fear, you're rewarded with peace and tranquility.

Kick Ass With Intentional Action | Your power is in choice. Don't give it away. Speak up when things are not as you desire and look after your own needs.

Day Three

"The truth is, unless you let go, unless you forgive yourself, unless you forgive the situation, unless you realize that the situation is over, you cannot move forward."

Steve Maraboli, Unapologetically You: Reflections on Life and the Human Experience

"Living my life from my own values, standards, and beliefs would be far more rewarding than blindly accepting someone else's."

Day 3

Reignite Your Core Beliefs

I stretched and opened my eyes slowly as the gong sounded. While I felt alert, I was slower getting up than the morning before. Once Veronica was done in the bathroom, I had a quick shower and headed to the meditation hall, grabbing a few pieces of foam from the landing at the top of the stairs. We had been warned that once we started Vipassana we were required to sit for one hour without moving. Working out the issues that would prevent me from doing that became my focus.

I used one piece of foam between my back and the wall. After leaning against it for hours at a time, the hardness of the surface became quite noticeable. Additionally, rather than crossing my legs into the traditional lotus position, I chose to place the soles of my feet together and shape my legs into a type of diamond shape. This was comfortable for long periods of time, but my anklebones made contact with the hardness of the floor. The second piece of foam solved that issue.

It took several minutes of primping and fluffing before I squatted to assume my meditation position. I closed my eyes, took a deep breath, and placed my attention on the area around my nose. *There's the breath coming in and going out. Coming in and going out. Coming in and going out. Coming in and going out. I'm cold. I think I need a blanket. I'll have to bring a blanket from my bed next time. I didn't feel cold a minute ago I was nice and warm while I moved around. Maybe I'll just move around. Oh crap—*

breath coming in and going out. Coming in and going out. The pattern continued between being able to focus my attention on the sensation of my breath and random thoughts popping into my head. I did find that the focused time seemed to be growing longer before my mind raced off on a tangent. I also found that there was less time before I became aware of the wandering thoughts and brought myself back to the attention on the breathing.

I continued to meditate and realized that I was not as tuned in to the noises around me in the room as I was the first morning. I felt like I was really getting into a great meditative state until I noticed I was actually falling asleep. It amazed me that I could feel alert and awake, and the moment I shut my eyes to meditate I was nodding off for naps. Yet, when I went to bed at night, when I wanted to drift off into slumber, my mind suddenly was churning with thoughts and ideas. It reminded me of when the twins were newborns. They were awake wanting to be fed all night and slept for long periods of the day. I remember telling my mom, "I think they have their days and nights mixed up." It seemed I had my meditation and sleep mixed up.

I woke with a start, straightening my slumped body. I'm not completely sure that I hadn't been snoring and roused myself in the middle of a snort. I decided to go back to my room and continue my meditation in a supine position. Which is code for, "I'm going back to bed and get some sleep." As I left the hall and tip-toed up the stairs, I guesstimated I was meditating for about an hour. Back in my room, the clock showed me that I was off by thirty minutes. It was 5:05 a.m. I crawled into bed. I put my sleep machine over my face, and my attention on my breathing for mere seconds before I was sound asleep.

The breakfast bell jolted me awake at 6:30. As I looked in the mirror, I could see the marks on my face where the straps from my mask had left an imprint. The good news was that no one was supposed to be looking at me, so they wouldn't know that I had been sleeping instead of meditating. The other good news was this morning I chose not to care whether anyone knew or not. The minute I made the choice, a smile burst from my face. A shift had occurred, and I felt free and weightless on the inside. I reveled in the moment a few minutes longer, thinking what a difference it would make in my life if I was able to have this perspective on a day-to-day basis.

How liberating it would be to live my life and not get caught in the drama of worrying what others thought of me—to put aside their judgments about the way that I should be, what I should do, and how I should act would save me a lot of apprehension. If I could focus my energies on me, concentrating on what I chose to do, be, and have, then that feeling of inner happiness would stay. Living my life from my own values, standards, and beliefs would be far more rewarding than blindly accepting someone else's.

I thought of Byron Katie's teachings. She says there are only three types of business—my business, your business, and God's business. When we focus on minding our own business, then we can lead a relatively stress-free life. We mentally get in someone else's business by judging what they need to do or how they should act. I realized that how someone else feels, what they say, or how they behave is totally out of my control. Similarly, the circumstances that are not within our control are God's business.

I had participated in a workshop where I learned about "The Work,"—Byron Katie's process of using four questions about a belief. Eventually, we change that belief by creating a turnaround statement. I reflected on a conversation that I had many years earlier and used that as the basis for working through this perspective changing process.

Stewart and I had been married for less than two years. We were living in his hometown, hanging with friends from his ball team, and spending time with his family. Both of us enjoyed our work. We had purchased our first home together and life was good.

Yet, something was missing. I felt like our relationship was not the intimate connection I had hoped it would be. One day, I reached my limit, and while we were having dinner together I blurted out my feelings. "I feel like you just don't love me enough; Like I am number five or six on your priority list. You are number one, your work is number two, your sports is number three, your family is number four, your friends are number five, and I come in around number six."

He was quiet as he sat across the table from me. I stared at the top of his head as he kept his eyes averted, studied his food, and contemplated his response. It felt like hours as I impatiently waited. I resisted my usual urge to keep talking and to demand an immediate answer. His response minutes later startled me. "Well, I will always be number one on my list and you will be number two. Just like on your list, you should be number one and I should be second."

My first reaction was: *You don't know anything about love, buddy.*

I felt deflated and hurt. I wanted him to say that I was the most important person in the world, that he loved me deeply, and he was willing to make me a priority. At the time, his total honesty really stung my ego. What I understood about love was that I was expected to give of myself—take care of my spouse and family. They came first. I came second. And I expected it to be that way with the man I had married.

As I used this example and did "The Work," on my belief that "my husband should love me more," my turnaround statement became, "I should love me more." That was a powerful, defining moment for me. Loving myself, taking care of myself, and doing what was right for me was totally my business and my choice. I can only control me and no one else. What others choose to think or feel about me is their business and I would be happier if I just stayed out of it!

Basking in the contentment of my early morning realization, that I really didn't care if anyone noticed the marks from my mask, I sauntered downstairs and into the kitchen. I filled my bowl with the steaming oatmeal. I thought of how Mom always made oatmeal cooked with Sunny Boy cereal that had flax, other grains, and a bit of a nutty flavour to it—and a really nice texture, a bit more like a thick soup than a ball of sticky paste. I looked into my bowl. This was not Mom's oatmeal. I added some rice milk, almonds, and brown sugar to make it more palatable. After cutting up my apple and orange at the island, I stepped back from the counter and crashed into someone behind me. A loud groan escaped my mouth before I had a chance to suppress it. In the silence it seemed much louder than it was, and it almost echoed in the room as all eyes turned to see what had broken the quiet. I almost blurted out "I'm sorry," but managed to close my mouth. *Maybe Dad was right when he joked that this would be a challenge for me.* This exchange was completely accidental, and I didn't feel like I broke the rules. Yet, I became aware that I am very conscious of rules and expectations.

I reflected on the rules and quickly thought of the term I loved from Vishen Lakhiani, the founder of Mindvalley. He talked about "Brules." These are the bullshit rules that we create in our minds from personal experiences and our upbringing from cultural, societal, and religious influences. I thought about the rules created for me, the ones I had created for myself and rules I had created for others. My life was filled with brules, and I wanted to change that.

These rules were cleverly disguised as: "I should," "I have to," and "I need to," based on judgments, expectations, and beliefs that I had acquired over my lifetime. They had become so ingrained in me that most times I was not even conscious of how they impacted my daily life. Deep in my subconscious mind was rule central, and it was time to challenge it, to release, and redefine the rules of my life. In that moment, I was determined to get rid of the coulda, shoulda, woulda way I had been living my life. I decided to stop "shoulding" on myself.

Not all things that I learned growing up were brules. There were lessons and values I was taught as well as observations and experiences that served me well. What did not serve me well was following expectations or rules that were in conflict with who I wanted to be—or with who I am. It dawned on me that when I was trying to live up to someone else's ideas of how and who I should be, I felt resentment. When I didn't live up to my own ideologies, I felt guilt and anger. The negativity built and fueled the misery that burned within me.

Among the most prominent rules that impacted my life were the roles and responsibilities with parenting. When my sister, Denise, had her first son, Joshua, the family gathered to celebrate, and I remember the accolades and support she received from our elders. Her decision to stay at home and not to work was the "right thing" to do, and she was being a "good mom" by putting her child's needs first.

When I had my own children, I too made the choice to become a stay-at-home mom. I quickly found out it would be the most difficult job that I would ever have. I had three bosses who demanded my time, energy, and emotions. The hours were long, and I didn't get to leave the work behind at the end of my shift—I was on call 24/7. Quite frankly, the pay sucked! I was totally dependent on Stewart's income for everything and felt like I had to ask permission to spend money. Relying on someone else financially had a drastic effect on my attachment to being an independent woman.

I became aware that when I was out, and people asked me what I did I replied, "I'm just a stay-at-home mom." By saying "just" I was discrediting that role, and it made me sad to think that was how I saw a time in my life that I thought I had always wanted. I certainly didn't recognize the benefits because I was caught up in the amount of work that needed to be done—cooking, cleaning, and changing diapers. I envied the mothers who were able to focus on the joy of raising and developing those little human beings. Opportunities for me to learn what the universe was trying to teach me happened on more than one occasion.

One year at the twins' birthday party, I was sitting among the group of kids and one of my neighbours said, "I thought Carla didn't like kids." Stew replied, "She likes the idea of kids."

I was mortified they were having that discussion and wanted to crawl to the corner, wallowing in humiliation. I interpreted their conversation that I didn't like kids; therefore, I didn't love my own children. *What kind of a mother doesn't love her own kids?* I do love my children deeply, and there were many great moments, but I hated doing some of the day-to-day work that went along with raising them.

Before I had kids, I had this grand vision of having a clean, well-organized home, preparing healthy nutritious food, happily playing and doing crafts with them, and loving every moment. It sounds more like a movie script or a rendition of the old-fashioned television show *Leave it to Beaver*. The vision couldn't have been further from the truth of what was happening. Most days, I was exhausted to the point where moving off the couch to accomplish something only happened in the half an hour before Stewart got home so he didn't see that I had "done nothing." I was going through the motions of life. Just doing what I had to do to get through the day.

Thank goodness some courageous moms wrote a book called, *I Was a Really Good Mom Before I Had Kids*. I felt like they told the story of my life—where the expectations and brules about what a "good mom" were debunked and they told the truth about reality. I didn't feel so alone when I read that book, and honestly, I was grateful that other mothers had struggles similar to my own. I was starting to understand that by sharing the truth of what it was really like, instead of saying the things we thought we should say, we could help others and build a support system.

Originally, I believed that my role as a stay-at-home mother was the root of my dissatisfaction. I thought resentment about giving up my professional career as a nurse was one of the reasons for my bitterness. Making that transition to be a mom wasn't easy, but the issue of sacrificing who I was had begun long before that.

It went back to when I first got married and was trying to be me when suddenly I was part of "we." In my life before kids, Stewart worked days and I was a shift worker. On days off I would catch up on cleaning and laundry. It's not as though he did nothing. He did clean up after himself. In our pre-marriage course, I had eagerly agreed that I would do all the typical "house duties," taking on responsibilities that both of us had witnessed as the wife's role. I was young, in love, and eager to please my husband. Little did I know then, I would resent that I unwittingly accepted the cultural roles rather than questioning whether that was how I wanted it to be.

One day as I put in the third load of laundry I applauded myself for how much I was getting done. Then it dawned on me: I was working on my days off, and Stewart was enjoying his time away from work riding bike, playing tennis, or hiking, while I was stuck inside. I resented him for not being there and helping with the household chores. But I hadn't asked him, nor had I created the opportunity for anything else to happen. I was angry with myself for taking on the role of housewife, as I had seen it done. I didn't ask for anything different. I got myself pretty twisted and bent out of shape so that when Stew came through the door feeling refreshed and content, I blasted him with my frustration. "I just hired a housekeeper. I'm tired of being the maid around here."

I spent a great deal of time feeling like I had a split personality. Part of me was trying to be like my mom—the epitome of housewives—and the other part was battling being a housewife.

I remember being in a counseling session and it was like a light bulb flashed. I said, "I really don't want to be 'Polly homemaker'." Even though I had numerous moments of clarity about who I didn't want to be, I continued on doing it for a long time because that was what was expected of me. It never occurred to me that I was the one that could choose differently. I tolerated responsibilities and a role that went against what I wanted because I was too attached to the expectations of others. In fact, I allowed others' beliefs and opinions to guide me, rather than taking ownership and stepping into the power of my own needs and wants.

The truth is I feared not being liked, accepted, and loved for who I truly was. That fear ran so deep that early on I learned to watch what I said or to act in a certain way so that I would gain approval of the people that I respected and loved. The adage, "Don't rock the boat" required me to conform to the norm rather than express my individual personality. And that meant I didn't need to expend any energy figuring out what that was. I could just learn the rules as determined by my parents or society and I would get along fine. Luckily, I have a bit of a rebellious streak in me, and eventually I found my voice and spoke out, even if it wasn't the popular thing to do. Ironically, here I was at a retreat where I wasn't saying anything at all, but the voice I was finding was one of my soul.

As I swallowed a spoonful of oatmeal, I glanced around the room—even though I was supposed to be completely focused on myself. I noticed that Amy, one of the participants I had talked to on the first day, was not there. I wondered if she slept in. When we entered the hall for the group sit, I scanned to see if Amy had moved. She wasn't there either. On the first day, she said that a friend she worked with had done the Vipassana retreat and came back seeming to be so calm and centered. Five of us sitting together shared a united time of uncertainty, wondering if we would make it to the end of the retreat. Now it seemed she was gone.

Instead of random thoughts popping up during that meditation, I thought of her leaving and questioned if I would make it. I wondered if I would feel compelled to quit. It was difficult to concentrate on the meditation as the questions whirled in my brain. I was pretty determined to stick it out to the end and was thinking this was one of those times that being stubborn might be useful.

I was deep in thought when the chanting started to end the session. "Cawla," the booming voice broke in. It startled me because it sounded like someone saying my name. I had a flash back to my grade eight science teacher, Mr. Kropinski, yelling at me because I wasn't paying attention. It made me smile to think that maybe all those years ago I had been meditating, but it was interpreted as not paying attention. Or, maybe I was just daydreaming. I resisted the urge to laugh out loud at the fond memory.

Looking for the humour in my surroundings became a theme that day. The atmosphere in the house felt somber with the silence. As I stood in line for lunch, I stifled my desire to share a story or make a witty remark. All of this meditating and personal reflection was hard work, and I felt laughter would lighten it.

Even before I arrived at the retreat, my revelation was that laughter, joy, and happiness were missing elements in my life. It wasn't as though they were completely absent. It simply felt like there was a dark cloud covering the light. The positive, upbeat, silly me had been replaced with an angry, resentful, and overly serious person I didn't even recognize. I wondered what the hell happened. After weaning myself off of antidepressants, I examined my life. I wasn't sure I liked the person I had become. I had been trying to impress others and gain their approval, and in the process, I had become someone I didn't really care much for. I could put on a mask to the outside world, act as if everything was great, and that I was happy and fun to be around. But what I couldn't hide from was the reflection in the mirror and the deep feelings that I was becoming increasingly aware of. It was a challenge to name the emotions because they were interspersed with thoughts and beliefs, some of which I didn't understand myself. Similar to when I was on the medication I still felt numbness—as though I was only going through the motions of life. My focus was on what I didn't have rather than what I did.

As I tried to determine when this downward spiral of negativity and unhappiness had begun, slowly the swirling clouds of misery separated long enough to show me glimpses of light.

Awareness of how I had been living my life led me to where I was at that moment in time. Awareness that, while I seemingly had it all, there was something missing. Awareness that what was missing was happiness, joy, and laughter. The only thing stopping me from that bliss was me. Somewhere along the line, I had stopped seeing the humour in life. I had started taking my life so seriously that rules, responsibilities, and expectations had squeezed out playfulness, enjoyment, and fun.

I heard depression defined as pressing down feelings, and it occurred to me that was what I had been doing for years. That was what led to a diagnosis of clinical depression and the medication to help me. But it hadn't helped me in the way that I wanted. Medication got me through the darkest hours, but what really started to show me the glimpses of light was having courageous conversations with myself, to process and express my emotions.

I recognized that when I started pushing my feelings away it wasn't just the so-called bad ones that I had distanced myself from, it was also the good ones. I tried to numb all feelings and stay in my head—be logical—so I could be strong. I was an expert at disconnecting and had been mastering that skill for years.

A month after my brother died I was with Mom cleaning 4-H calves and preparing them for a show. Our family had decided to donate Dale's calf to raise money for a cause. It was cold that day, but the hot water from the pressure washer and scrubbing the soap into a thick lather kept my hands warm. I remember feeling agitated, and I couldn't quite put my finger on what was bothering me, but I knew I didn't want to be there. I wanted to be alone and not be outside working. Then, I became aware of a pain in my lower abdomen—subtle at first but the more I focused on it the more intense it became. Soon I was doubled over and crying. I think Mom was frustrated because there was work to do, but I managed to get out of it. The pain and the hysteria built and carried on into the night until she decided to take me to the hospital.

I was admitted that night and given medication for the pain. I settled in and Mom stayed at my bedside for a long time before leaving for home. I remember feeling closeness with my mom that I had been longing for. The nurses checked on me through the night, and in the morning a long battery of tests was started to determine what was causing pain that had me writhing and crying. The days added up, and I fell into the hospital routine with ease, waiting in bed for whatever procedure I would be having that day. It was more like a glamorous vacation in-between the episodes of drama. I was content and enjoyed the visits from concerned family. Dad picked fresh pussy willows and sent them in with Mom. This attention from my parents made me feel special and loved.

My boyfriend, would come every day after school for clandestine visits. Even though I was not allowed to go out on dates, holding hands and making out in the back of the volleyball team bus meant I was going steady. I was pretty impressed that I had the affections of an older guy and was happy to have the opportunity for the teenage romance. Being in the hospital meant spending more time with him. I remember sitting in the visitor's area or my hospital room and just talking. I don't think we held hands or even kissed. What I do recall was how it made me feel to have someone be present and there for me.

The nurses doted on me, and the doctor had concerned discussions with my parents. He had run every test possible at our small town and found nothing physically to explain my situa[illegible] The attacks, as we had started to call them, were still happenin[illegible] Not once do I remember being afraid or concern for myself. In fact, I was relishing in the attention I was getting.

The physician decided to send me to the big city hospital—more concern, more attention, and more time with Mom. In the days and weeks following Dale's death, we picked ourselves up, dusted ourselves off and carried on the best that we knew how. We were all individuals living in the same house but detached from each other emotionally. I craved love and nurturing from my parents. But I couldn't ask for it. I didn't know how. And at that time, they couldn't give it, because they were trying to deal with their own devastation and grief. The best that they knew how to do was to be strong. So unconsciously, I found a way to get what I needed. Physical pain couldn't be ignored. Physical pain had to be investigated. Physical pain was more tangible.

After a week of more tests in the city, I was diagnosed. Psychosomatic pain caused by grief. I was discharged and told that there was nothing "physically wrong with me" so when the attacks came I had to ignore them until they went away. The pain was often at its worst during the quiet, before I slept, so Mom spent many nights rubbing my back, reiterating the message from the doctor to just ignore the pain. *Welcome to Detaching from Your Emotions 101!*

As years went on, rather than expressing negative emotions, I suppressed them as I had learned to do in that early moment in my life. Another rule that surfaced from childhood was, "If you don't have anything nice to say, don't say anything at all." So, there I was, feeling overwhelmed with not-so-nice feelings about myself, my situation, and my life, believing I had to keep quiet.

When bad thoughts or feelings continuously bubbled to the surface, I disguised them as humour. Attempts to make people laugh had been fraught with sarcasm and self-deprecating

a dark form of joking that attempted to release
side. Making jokes had become a way to deflect
s a way to avoid being vulnerable.
the type of laughs or attention I wanted. I
laughter that caused tears to roll down my
and, made me feel happy on the inside. Incorporating more fun and enjoyment in my life and finding time for silly, giddy feel good moments became even more important for me. It wasn't that they were not there. I just didn't recognize them because I was focusing on the wrong things. And I wanted to be seen for who I was…but perhaps I wasn't even seeing myself. Looking back, because I wasn't seeing myself, I drew attention to myself in unlikable ways.

When I was a new bride, a regular comment from Stewart's acquaintances and people I met was that I was so lucky to be married to him. It is true that he was a really nice guy (which is why I chose him) but *what I heard* from the repeated statement was that I was not worthy of such a great guy. It played on my shaky self-esteem and the belief that I was not good enough. I'm not proud of the way I chose to respond to those feelings of inadequacy. One of my regrets through that time was how I treated Stew. We were well known for the sparring we would do at parties. The bold truth is I became a bully. I used sarcasm and put downs, and I tried to gloss it over with humour. In a twisted way I thought that if others knew about his flaws, somehow that would make me feel better about mine. After all, he was pretty damn lucky to be married to me! Why didn't anyone mention that?

For so many years, I placed the blame on him for what he said or didn't say that really hurt my feelings. I didn't speak up to ask for what I wanted or openly share my thoughts and emotions. I tried to hide them, but they had the most alarming way of surfacing when we were out in public, and I would jokingly bring up an issue to garner support for my case.

When it came right down to it, I hadn't really stopped to figure out what it was I did want so I could create it.

In the last several years, I had taken a look at my life and made some changes. I processed some of those feelings I had held in for so long. I was willing to let go of long-held beliefs and take back my personal power. Most importantly, I recognized I wanted to be loved, appreciated, and accepted. I was basing my happiness on those needs. To me the laughter and humour were the outward signs of joy. When I was living from the inside out—loving, appreciating, and accepting myself the laughter was genuine, heartfelt, and true. Like little bubbles of champagne rising to the surface when you released the cork.

All those memories came flooding back as I took my position on my cushions. I sat painfully still in the darkened room. The quiet of the retreat felt like a pressure valve had been installed and with no speaking there needed to be some kind of energy release. I stifled a giggle and a smile broke out on my face when I thought of instituting a laugh out loud moment in my day-to-day life—just not for the next seven days. In the meantime, I created humorous scenarios and comments in my head to balance the long hours of meditation. Little did I know that the Universe was going to provide me with a little bit of humour during the evening discourse.

Goenka used stories to illustrate his teachings. He had a dry wit, and I could see a little sparkle in his eye as he shared a tale. Goenka's story to illustrate attachment was quite amusing when he described a husband seeing his wife's beautiful hair and commenting on her hair, "Oh, what beauty." That is until he finds it in his dinner, and becomes indignant, "What is this dirty hair in my food?" His facial expressions, his emphasis, and the way he told the story provided me with that laugh out loud opportunity I had been craving. He told another story of one boy trying to describe the color white to a blind friend that continued the amusement. When I first heard myself laugh, it felt foreign because it broke the silence. It was such a natural response and I did notice that others were chuckling with me. I felt like I had the loudest reaction and was totally okay with that because that is exactly what I needed in that moment!

As I left the meditation hall that evening, I recognized that the day ended in the same way it began, with insights that made me feel good. I smiled to myself as I turned the light off and crawled into bed, feeling lighter and happier.

Simple Steps to Reignite Your Core Beliefs

Stir Your Soul | Loving yourself, taking care of yourself and doing what's right for you is totally your choice and your business. Making yourself a priority is the surest way to be happy to serve others.

Power Up Your Potential | Bring back playfulness and fun to your life. Don't allow rules, responsibilities and expectations squeeze them out.

Activate Your Awareness | Challenge, release and redefine your Rules—which are cleverly disguised as "should's", "have to's", and "need to's"—and be mindful of "justs", which diminish you and your accomplishments.

Rock Your Resilience | Find the humour in one of the rules you've uncovered in your belief system. The next time the old belief comes up, give yourself a laugh over it.

Kick Ass With Intentional Action | Schedule some "me" time for yourself this week and stick to it. Spending the time doing whatever makes you happy.

Day Four

"God grant me the serenity to accept the people I cannot change, the courage to change the one I can, and the wisdom to know it's me."

Adaptation of "The Serenity Prayer"

"Suddenly, I felt calm, and excited, almost giddy. I tuned out the internal chatter and released my attachment to the fear. I was totally in the moment."

Day 4

Reignite Your Courage

I awoke minutes before the morning gong. I had a flash to Bill Murray in the movie *Groundhog Day* where he keeps waking up and repeating his day from start to finish. I felt a strong resistance to rise and shine. The restless nights I continued to experience were wreaking havoc with my energy level. I closed my eyes, fighting the urge to fall back asleep. Finally, I dragged myself from my warm and comfortable bed. Climbing into a hot and steamy shower, I applauded myself for sticking to the commitment of early morning waking. Even if it was short lived. After a forty-minute meditation in the hall, I returned for my pre-breakfast nap.

Following the usual morning meal of sticky oatmeal, I sat in my same spot on the couch in the corner watching the sky lighten and bring on the day. I was excited that there would be a change in our meditation practice. I was ready to get going on the Vipassana technique. I allowed a moment of impatience to sneak in before I decided that if I relaxed and allowed the process to unfold, it would be more enjoyable.

In the evening discourse the night before, Goenka had reminded us that the first three days had only been preparation, training the mind to concentrate. *I'm not sure I fulfilled that skill of concentration. The random thoughts and ideas seem endless.* He had also warned us that now the hard work would begin as we started Vipassana and moved toward pañña or wisdom. *NOW the hard work would begin… what the hell has the last three days been?*

It was hard work trying to train this crazy mind of mine. It was hard work to stay quiet. It was hard work dissecting my life! Holy shit if the hard work is just about to begin—what have I gotten myself into?

We had been practicing Anapana meditation where we focused our attention on the sensation of our breath in the small area in and around our nose. Goenka had not yet shared the technique of Vipassana. And because I didn't feel as though I had mastered the concentration during Anapana, I was apprehensive to be moving on to a new process.

As part of the previous days teachings, our guru outlined three levels of wisdom. The first stage was when we read or heard information and ideas from leaders and teachers. This stage definitely gives us inspiration and guidance. But in order to move to the next level, we must examine the teachings intellectually to determine if they are logical and pragmatic. *Aha, this is where we determine the brules! Seems pretty straight forward.* The final stage of wisdom is moving to purification of the mind and experiencing it for ourselves. *I don't get it! What am I purifying my mind of? I'm not sure what I will be experiencing, but I hope I get to this stage of wisdom.*

Stage one and two of wisdom had become a part of the self-discovery that I had been working on prior to the retreat. I was comfortable with that. But I worried that I wouldn't be able to get to the final stage in the next seven days. It felt like there wasn't enough time. Anxiety rose in me as I recognized that need to achieve, to get it right, and to experience the feelings. Goenka shared that direct experience would help us come out of the misery and find deep peace and happiness—and that's what I was at this retreat to do. *I hope I recognize it when I experience it.*

I took a deep breath as my awareness came back to the dining room and noted the sunrise I had been observing had passed while I was lost in thought. Just as the sun had moved on, I was really ready for a change. The schedule was exactly the same each day, so I looked for opportunities to make something different. That morning I decided to brave the bitter cold and take a walk in the yard. The expansive enclosure was split down the middle with rope strung between stakes. One side for the women and the other for the men. I followed the beaten path in the snow, created by others who had been out in the days before. The frosty air caught in my throat and burned my nostrils, but I was determined to make one lap around. Even here, there was silence except for the crunching sound my steps made in the crusty snow. I smiled as I walked through a slushy patch and wondered if the other women realized they were crossing the septic field. I carried on around the perimeter but decided to cut a new path where no one had gone before. With my first few steps, I sunk up to mid-shin, and the deep-crusted snow scraped my bare skin as my pant leg got pushed up above my boot. *Hmm that hurt. Keep moving and get back to the path.* The little detour allowed me to choose a new path, feel like I had control, and reminded me that it's not always easy to do so.

Walking that morning felt good despite the icy wind that penetrated my clothing and stung my skin. I was compelled to stay out and do another lap before retreating to the warmth of the house. Maybe it was the cold and maybe it was the fact that I was moving, but I felt totally invigorated. In that moment, I felt a sense of gratitude. Like my walk, I had started making choices in my life that sometimes took me off the beaten track. While it had been challenging, each time I ventured out I grew stronger and more resilient. I liked change. That day as I felt stuck in the routine of the retreat schedule I welcomed the different technique we would be learning.

Our eight-a.m. meditation was the first sit of what was referred to as strong determination. The instructions were simple yet challenging. For one hour we were to remain perfectly still with eyes, hands, and feet closed. That meant no adjusting positions to stretch out a cramp, no scratching the inevitable itch on your face, and avoiding the urge to shift your weight off your numb butt cheek. Hence, strong determination because squirming and moving were all tactics used while sitting for long periods of meditation—at least they were the ones I had been using.

Fortunately, I had a task for my mind, to distract me from my desire to move my body. The practice of Vipassana was described as the, "observation of sensations throughout the body, the experiential understanding of their changing nature, and the development of a balanced mind by learning not to react to them." The strategy was to start at the top of my head and observe for any sensations, methodically moving awareness down my body toward my toes and noticing any and all sensations. My long-held practice of ignoring feelings and sensations in my body would make this a challenge—or so I thought.

I imagined an MRI scanning my body to identify not an image but a feeling. As I focused on each area I did feel sensations, but generally not in that spot. When I put attention on my ears I noticed a tingle in my nostril that made me want to sneeze. As I moved to my face the spasm in my bicep grabbed my consideration. By the time I arrived at my arms, I perceived the tiniest itch on my cheek (not the numb one). There was no shortage of sensations; the test became not to respond to them. By concentrating on not attending to them with movement, scratching, or rubbing, I was able to recognize that they went away on their own. The other realization I had was that if I stopped and focused on a sensation like an itch, it would intensify; but, if I continued on with the scan in the way that I was instructed, it faded more quickly.

I couldn't help but draw a connection between that method of awareness and how I had approached my life. I was struck by how easily my attention could be drawn away, like the dog in the movie *Up* when he heard someone say "squirrel." I had a tendency to be impatient and impulsive. I often created stories or drama in my life by reacting to something someone said or didn't say. I acted out or had outbursts and said things in the moment that brought chaos into my life. If I had paused, relaxed, and observed, rather than reacted, I could have had more harmony. The other link I made was with the sensations and how they dissolved. Like the emotions I had tried to suppress for so long, I recognized that if I did not resist them and simply allowed them to surface they would pass rather than continuing to bubble to the surface and intensify to the boiling point.

As the chanting signaled the end of the hour, I was relieved and delighted that I had remained still during the entire session. I was also pretty psyched that I had felt sensations, even if they weren't in the applicable places as I moved through the scanning process. I would be lying if I said that I didn't have minutes where my mind wandered to random thoughts, but they didn't dominate. I quite liked that I had a technique that I could return to my focus. It took me a while to scan from the top of my head to my toes as thoughts would enter, and I would get distracted before coming back to scanning.

At the end of the meditation, we were given the opportunity to continue in the hall or in our own place. I chose to return to my room and laid on the bed to practice the new method. Happily, I didn't fall asleep, but I did find it more difficult to stay committed to the scanning for sensations as I got caught up with my earlier thoughts. During my musings that morning, I had decided that I liked change, but that was not true of all aspects of my life. In some areas there was a strong resistance to change. And in a few parts, there was a downright block to moving forward and making progress. I struggled most with removing unhealthy eating habits and incorporating the disciplines of exercise, which I knew were essential to taking care of myself. *There's another area of personal growth I'm going to have to uncover!*

As I pondered this, I reflected on another time that I had been led through the *Tree of Life Meditation.* We were being guided through a process of focusing on sensations in different parts of the body, and up to that time I had never felt or experienced anything resembling a sensation. I was totally caught off guard when we placed our attention on the right hip area and I felt a sudden ache like the muscle was going into a spasm. I nearly shouted out loud. I was so excited that I noticed something and instantly wanted to know what that meant. As the leader continued, he explained that this area of the body was associated with moving forward in life. That sensation indicated a block or a resistance to progress and change in a forward direction. Yet, I knew that I had made a lot of personal changes and was thinking and feeling so much better than when I was treated for depression and even when I came off the medication. *How is it that I could feel like I had come so far and at the same time felt like I had so far to go?*

I heard somewhere that in order to grow you need to do three things: First, find out what's working and continue doing it. Second, find what's not working and stop doing it. And third, try new things. This seemed like sound advice and a simple concept. Maybe too simple. I had been trying new things. *A ten-day meditation retreat was pretty unusual, right?* And continuing on with the things that seemed to be going well was pretty easy. The challenge was in stopping things that were not in my best interest. I continued to do them anyway. Like overeating, not exercising or watching too much television. In general, not being committed to my own well-being. Intellectually, I knew that they weren't working for me, and I should eat less, exercise more, and turn the mind numbing shows off. *Oooh, there's the 'should' word again! It is not about what I should do but what I choose to do or wanted to do. Why am I not choosing to care for myself? Why do I not want to do the things that will move me forward? What is the procrastination to do things? If I'm so happy to have change, what is stopping me from making the changes in these areas? I have more questions than answers and the biggest question of all was how is scanning my body for sensations going to help me get the answers?*

Some change is natural and happens without resistance. Yet, it struck me that certain change takes courage. In the past year and a half, I had been in several group activities where members had described me as courageous. I didn't consider this as an attribute of mine and wondered what they saw that I didn't. I had them fooled, because if I stopped to pay attention to what I was feeling—it was fear. Varying degrees of fear usually directly proportional to the degree of risk or the amount of change was required to get the results I wanted. I realized that the fear of being sad and depressed, of not feeling joy and laughter, was a bigger fear than trying to forge ahead and resolve the thoughts and beliefs that were getting in the way of my happiness.

Probably my biggest fear was the leaving a less than stellar legacy for my kids. Sometimes I was in touch with this emotion, but most times I just charged ahead and didn't put much thought into it.

Nelson Mandela's quote seemed particularly appropriate for my thoughts in that moment. "I learned that courage was not the absence of fear, but the triumph over it. The brave man is not he who does not feel afraid, but he who conquers that fear."

I wouldn't say I had conquered one of my greatest frights, but I had certainly stared it down and moved through it. Or maybe I should say up it. When I was hired as an Emergency Response Officer, I was trained as a fire fighter, which complimented my nursing expertise. *This is pretty cool!* What wasn't cool was that in order to complete my certification I had to climb to the top of the 105-foot aerial ladder. In the interview, I had been asked about claustrophobia, but not about a fear of heights.

I stood at the base of the ladder on top of pumper five and tipped my head back to look up. My head fell back with the weight of my helmet. *Damn that's high.* I squinted as I looked into the blue sky and directly into the sun. I was perspiring like I had just come out of a sauna. I wasn't sweating profusely because I was wearing full fire bunker gear on a hot day. I was cold and clammy because I was terrified! *That should be Terrified with a capital T.*

I had been given all the safety training and was being coached by the four guys on my shift. My senior officer Clark was going to follow a few paces behind me to support the climb. I thought the first few rungs I moved pretty quickly considering it felt like my limbs were made of cement. The further up away from the truck, I slowed dramatically. I focused on my breathing, which was shallow and rapid so I had to concentrate to slow it down. My neck was straining from looking up at the bucket. I dared not look down and looking straight ahead did nothing to calm me as I realized how high off the ground I was. I put my attention on the destination and slowly climbed one rung at a time. I could feel the ladder swaying slightly in the wind the higher I got. At first this totally freaked me out then something shifted in me.

Suddenly, I felt calm, and excited, almost giddy. I tuned out the internal chatter and released my attachment to the fear. I was totally in the moment. I realized I was climbing the ladder and I was closer to the top than I was to the bottom. I had not fallen (which was really the greatest fear), and this was an experience I would remember for the rest of my life. I wouldn't say the last thirty feet was a breeze, but they were more enjoyable than the start. When I relaxed into it, there was a drastic improvement in that experience. The panoramic view from the bucket was the industrial site where we worked, but it might have been the Grand Canyon for how much I reveled in it. At that moment I felt like I had kicked fear's ass, and I could do anything—except climb down. We lowered the bucket and the training exercise was completed. My confidence and mind were strong. My legs on the other hand felt like they were made of jelly!

Reminiscing made me smile as the gong sounded for lunch. While the menu was different at each lunch, the group had established an unspoken routine. We would line up and move the same direction around the island, most people sat in the same spot or area of the table and then retire to either the couch or their rooms. Each meal felt quite repetitious. After eating, I again went to look out the window, but I chose a different place on the couch. The lady that normally sat there hesitated for a moment before moving to a chair. No words or looks were exchanged, but I could tell that I had interrupted more than just my own habit pattern. I resisted the urge to say sorry to her.

I felt restless. I really wanted to have a conversation with somebody beside myself. I debated about putting my name on the list to meet with the teacher. Once per day we were allowed to request an audience with Sharon if we had questions about the technique. I pictured the whole conversation in my head. I walk solemnly into the room, kneel on the pillow in front of her and instead of my whispery meditation hall tone, in my regular loud voice say, "*Hey Sharon, how's the retreat going for you? I'm a bit restless and don't really have a question I just needed to hear my voice to be sure I could still talk. I'm really liking it here and doing a lot of deep thinking about my life. I seem to be catching up on my sleep during the morning meditation times cause I'm sure as hell not sleeping at night. Otherwise things are going pretty well. Sharon, did you know that out in the yard we are walking through the sewer? Oh, and by the way the meals are good, but the morning oatmeal is pretty gross, don't ya think?*" At which point in my fantasy, I would let her get a word in and get my admonishment for using the time inappropriately. I wondered if she would crack a smile. I would giggle, leave the room, and return to sit in my same spot on the couch having released my rant out loud. I wondered, if those were the crazy little stories I was creating on day four, what would my imagination have in store by day ten!

The afternoon sit of strong determination was uneventful. I continued with the scanning and successfully sat without moving.

I was not yet feeling sensations in the particular focus areas of the body. I was feeling what was referred to as gross sensations—pain, pressure, an itch or twitch, but nothing subtle reached my awareness. I did have to tell myself not to get frustrated. After all, I had perfected the technique of ignoring my body and my feelings over a period of thirty years, I couldn't expect that I could flip a switch and it would all come back to me.

Since I had enjoyed my walk outside that morning, I decided to venture out again before teatime. To my delight I noticed that someone else had taken my little detour and the snow had been beaten down a bit. This time it was easier leaving the path and the early evidence of a new trail was starting to form. On that particular walk I concentrated on taking a break from thinking and analyzing and to notice what I was sensing in my body and my surroundings. I felt the freshness of the air as it entered my nose and my lungs. I heard the crunch of the snow under my feet, but this time I also heard the vehicles from the highway about a mile away. I saw the blinding glare as the sun shone on the glistening snow. I tried to bring my awareness back in to my body instead of externally. My cheeks were tingling from the cold and my hands were starting to feel a little numb. I applauded myself for tuning in and returned to the house for the last sit of the day before our evening discourse.

Goenka started in the same way as always, "The fourth day is over, you have six more days to go." He then expressed that this was an important day because we started the study of Vipassana. We were told this was a peculiar technique and different than many other styles of meditation. Often there is a mantra, chanting of a word or a phrase used to concentrate the mind. Sometimes people use an image of God or religious object to hold their attention. These teachings suggest that other meditation techniques are good for that and when you achieve it you will find that a change has started. Goenka suggested that the change is just at the surface level, in the conscious level of the mind. But the problems lie in the unconscious mind and that is where the root cause of our unhappiness is stored. As he put it, "From the time one has taken birth and opened one's eyes you are seeing things outside all the time. The outside things have been so predominant you never cared to know what was happening inside. Even if you tried to meditate with closed eyes you worked with objects outside—visualization, words, what was heard and seen, and you never tried to observe the reality as it is within the framework of the body."

Goenka pointed out that the reality is constantly changing. In the days that would follow we would develop a sharpness of the mind to experience subtle sensations on every part of the body from our head to feet. I wanted to put my hand up and say, "Yes, but how does feeling the sensations on the body translate into getting to the root cause of our misery?" *I do believe that there is a mind-body connection and our thoughts can impact how we feel, but how will feeling sensations help with the process of purification?*

Next came the biology lesson with a twist I'd not thought of before. Our guru explained that our entire physical structure is made of tiny subatomic particles. *I know this from high school biology and nursing.* Goenka's next statement caught my attention "There is no solidity in the material world." Our sensations and the subtle reality that he kept referring to, were the vibration and movement of these *kalāpās*—tiny particles. He expressed that "If you want to understand the law of nature at the deeper level, you must have direct experience of the law of the nature." Meaning, experience the subtle vibrations that were constantly changing.

The clarity I was craving started to come as the lesson continued. Besides the physical body we learned about the four major portions or aggregates of the mind. The first is the conscious part of the brain whose job is to receive the information. This is done through our six senses—everything we hear, see, smell, taste, touch, and think. Perception, the second part of the mind, jumps in to recognize the stimuli, evaluates it using previous experiences, memories and interpretations giving it meaning. As soon as the evaluation is complete, the third stage is a sensation or subtle vibration in the body. The fourth stage is the reaction of the mind within the unconscious. Goenka explained that we have been mentally conditioned to react to all of these stimuli. He called the reactions *saṅkhāra*. The example was that if I hear words, I interpret these based on my experiences and memories. If they are good words, I get a nice sensation. If they are negative or words of abuse, I get a negative sensation. The reaction of the mind is to say I want more of the good so I create a craving or a clinging for more of that. If not so good, I create an aversion or hating. And according to Goenka, it is our attachment to these cravings or aversions that creates the misery in our lives.

So the practice of Vipassana is to develop the capability of the mind to be so focused that we will feel these subtle sensations on the body. The second part is to learn to recognize it, and not react to it thus creating a *saṅkhāra*. In the next six days we would train to change the habit of the mind to feel the sensations and not react. Goenka closed the discourse by encouraging us to make the best use of our opportunity to come out of the misery, to come out of the ignorance of generating *saṅkhāras* and be liberated to enjoy real peace, real harmony, and real happiness.

As I walked back to my room I pondered that I always enjoyed the evening discourses, however, it generated so much processing of the information it took me a long time to settle down. While the lights were out at 9:30 p.m., it was long after that before my mind was ready for sleep.

Simple Steps to Reignite Your Courage

Stir Your Soul | Appreciate your body, with all of its imperfections, and the many things it allows you to do. Be grateful for the signals it sends to your mind and heart to help you stay balanced, focused, healthy.

Power Up Your Potential | In order to grow, remember these three simple things: recognize what's working in your life and keep doing it; recognize what's not working in your life and stop doing it.; and, try new things.

Activate Your Awareness | Adopt a habit of pausing, observing, and responding rather than reacting to the events that occur around you, and you will enjoy more harmony in your life.

Rock Your Resilience | Realize that there's a connection between your body and mind. Allow discomfort and negative thoughts and feelings to simply be, and they will dissipate much faster.

Kick Ass With Intentional Action | Close your eyes and focus inward on what you're feeling in your body. If there are any sensations that come up, ask your body to tell you what it needs in that moment, and then give it.

Day Five

"Find the love you seek, by first finding the love within yourself. Learn to rest in that place within you that is your true home."

Sri Sri Ravi Shankar
Spiritual Leader and Humanitarian

"If I wanted to make the change to healthy disciplines and loving self-care, it would start with the mental action of loving and appreciating myself, being compassionate, and kicking the bully's ass to the curb. It was time."

Day 5

Reignite Your Compassion

Hump day in meditation land. I had made it to the half way point, and while I remained restless that morning, I was pleased with myself that I had endured the quiet. I had been progressing and was starting to enjoy the technique I was learning. What I hadn't embraced was the gong sounding at four in the morning. I had created an aversion to it, and the enthusiasm of the first mornings was gone. It would have been a whole lot easier not to react in a negative way if I had been getting a nice restorative sleep. My nights were filled with tossing, turning, and long periods of lying awake processing information from the day before.

That morning I was experiencing what marathon runners refer to as the middle miles. I have never done a marathon, and I don't consider myself a runner—but I had once run a 10K. All because of Oprah, wine and my big mouth. While consuming more than a healthy amount of wine, I told my sister-in-law, JoAnn that "Oprah says everyone should run a 5K race." I was stunned two weeks later when she called and told me she'd signed us up for "Melissa's Road Race." When I squealed, "What the hell did you do that for?" she told me that I claimed everyone should run a race. I retorted, "NO! Oprah says everyone should run a race, not me!" "And a 5K not a 10K." Suddenly, I heard myself agreeing to a 10K, elite race in the Canadian Rockies. Initially, I was reluctant, but became enthusiastic once I started my preparations, which were delayed since I was recovering from a hysterectomy.

As the race approached I was ready and eager to get it done. I had gone from only being able to run for thirty seconds to running for fifteen minutes at a stretch before walking for five minutes. I was proud of the accomplishment but the training time in the middle was full of drudgery and frustration. The day of the race came and the four of us who had signed up together were all filled with nervous excitement. The energy at the start line was palpable. After running for ten minutes, I noticed the crowd thinned out, and everyone settled into their own pace. My pace was that of a turtle and I assumed my place at the back of the crowd, as I was sucking wind and had to walk. My planned fifteen and five intervals turned into five minutes run, five minutes huff and puff, three minutes shuffle, two minutes of barely faster than standing still. I wished I hadn't put double knots in my laces, so I could use the excuse to stop and tie my shoes. Those middle miles were a struggle! First, I hadn't planned on running at this elevation and air was thinner in the mountains. Second, I had trained on a flat track and a quarter mile into the race we ran up a mountain (the grade of the hill was probably nine percent, but still!). Third, I found it really tedious and boring to just run when something wasn't chasing me. Maybe I was missing the point and I'm sure that many runners would tell me so. I never got to the runners high that I have heard people talk about. I was focusing on the struggle and difficulty instead of on the experience of being in my first race in an absolutely beautiful location with people on the sidelines cheering us on.

I found renewed energy as I came into the last kilometer and picked up my stride, pulled my shoulders back, and realized I was going to finish the race. It helped that the athletes who were running the half and the full marathon crossed paths here and total strangers were patting me on the back and giving words of encouragement as they carried on and I made the turn to the final stretch. Crossing the finish line was a total rush. I basked in the feelings of accomplishment, relief, and pride. I even had to wipe away a few tears. My goal was to finish the race in a vertical position, before the event was over, and not require any medical attention before, during or after. Mission accomplished.

As I lay in bed that morning, that tedious and bored feeling of the in between which I had experienced in the race, came over me as day five started. The beginning had been exciting, and I was looking forward to the accomplishment at the end, but these days in the middle were uneventful as I practiced this meditation technique. Prior to the retreat I had expectations that this would be the final frontier to discover and clear the blocks to contentment and happiness. I had many scattered thoughts and memories that came up, but not anything I considered inspired answers. Maybe I was waiting for some grand gesture or a movie moment where the heavens open up, and there is a definitive sign from above and all the answers were downloaded into my conscious mind. That would be easier *and way more dramatic.*

That morning I decided not to go to the hall and remained in bed to catch some much-needed rest. I threw my covers over my head as I realized that for years when I slept in I would hear my dad's voice in my head telling me, "You're missing the best part of the day." That voice had been replaced by the advice from Goenka the night before about making the best use of the opportunity. I didn't have the energy to listen to any voices, and I didn't have the energy to get out of bed and do more meditating. There would be time for that after breakfast.

Two hours later, feeling much more refreshed, I awoke and had time for a quick shower before heading downstairs for breakfast. I was surprised at how alert I felt, and my mind immediately started to mull over an analogy that Goenka had used the night before. I knew with the impact it had on me the night before it needed more of my attention.

The *saṅkhāras* that we create have varying degrees of impact on our lives. He equated the strength and quality of our cravings and aversion on three levels. If you draw a line in the water with your finger it diminishes almost immediately. I thought of little irritations that I experienced in my daily life like being frustrated with other drivers, waiting in line for coffee at Tim Hortons, or trying to get the kids up for school. The deeper *saṅkhāra* was like drawing a line in the sand—it stays until later in the day when it is washed away with the tide. But the deepest line was drawn in the rock with a chisel and hammer. These were the most damaging, lasted the longest, and sometimes took years to eradicate. I wondered if I would get to the bedrock of my subconscious mind, and if I did, wondered if I would be able to heal those deep wounds etched there.

I had a moment of clarity when I reflected on the messages from the night before. He described our three types of actions: physical, vocal, and mental. I had a tendency to focus all my attention on what I was saying and doing, but as it was pointed out, everything starts in the mind. "The vocal and physical is nothing but a measure of the mental action," Goenka stated. I already knew that thoughts become beliefs and those impacted my behaviours, but somehow that morning it sunk in that my impure mind was creating my misery. My experiences were a projection of my mind. I had years of demonizing notions to transform if I wanted to find the happiness I was looking for. I also realized it is not the things I said out loud that were so damaging; it was the voice in my head that created the chaos. *Everyone has an inner critic—mine was a big nasty bully.*

I reflected on the bullying campaigns in schools and in the media and wondered if any of these focused on the root cause. I contemplated my own situation and came to the realization that while I was wreaking havoc on myself internally, I was projecting that on to Stewart and the kids. I went from periods of emotional detachment and withdrawal to lashing out in anger or frustration. It was like a rollercoaster ride because interspersed with the pessimism would be moments when I actually felt happiness.

However, my predominant thoughts and feelings definitely ranged in the negative realm. When I was seeing the psychiatrist, and I described a rough week she would up my medication. If I came in and talked about being happy or something good in my life, she asked me if I thought I was bi-polar swinging from depression to mania. I remembered thinking; *one mental illness is enough for me, thanks. Let's just deal with the depression.* And in the end, the depression was just a label and the medication was not the answer.

Even though I was diagnosed with depression in my thirties, the mental abuse from my bully had started years earlier. The idea of not disappointing others, wanting to be loved, being appreciated and acknowledged, as well as setting impossibly high standards for myself and others all contributed to the downward spiral into negativity. I was looking for all of this on the outside when where I really needed the acceptance, the appreciation, and the love was on the inside. I was waiting for someone else to say it and show it—and all the while that someone needed to be me.

As I stared out the window in my usual post breakfast routine, I continued meandering through my memories and thought of the marriage counselling sessions that Stew and I had attended, after a particularly stressful time in our life. It was a six-month period of living on our driveway in a tent trailer with three small children and spending outrageous amounts of money on an extreme home makeover while trying to carry on a normal work, school, and social life. We also had night-time visits from bears to amplify the stress. When it was all over, we were settled in my dream home, where I had everything I wanted when I suddenly realized there was a problem between Stew and me. We were barely talking to each other. There was major tension between us, and we didn't have the energy to try and fix it ourselves. We agreed to attend a session with a counsellor. I was thrilled. I planned to go right from the beginning of our relationship and share all of the ways he had let me down, not been attentive, not loved me enough, and had said hurtful things. I had a whole laundry list of complaints, wounds, and finger-pointing to get off my chest.

We had two sessions. In the first one, he shared that he was annoyed that I hadn't taken the renovation debt seriously, kept on spending money that we didn't have, and joked about it with other people. In both appointments, I had done my best to make him out to be the bad guy, even providing hard evidence in the form of examples and stories. It was in the second session the counsellor shared her observations and suggested that I take a look at my low self-esteem. Instead of booking further sessions (and spending more money on counselling) we left, Stewart feeling as though we had accomplished what he needed and me reeling with the idea that I had some work to do. As I reflected on that memory, I felt gratitude. That was the impetus for the personal growth journey that had led me to this ten-day silent retreat. In the silence, maybe I was finding the answers that had long eluded me.

My musings had followed me through the usual morning fare of sticky oatmeal and on to the sofa. Now it was time to take a break from the deep thoughts and head to the meditation hall. I took a few moments to find my most comfortable position for the hour of stillness ahead. In order to focus, I found myself repeating the body part where I was searching for sensations. *Top of the head, top of the head, top of the head. Oh, there's an itch beside my eye.* This carried on all the way down my body, placing my awareness on one part of my body only to be feeling something somewhere totally different. And then it happened. After about forty minutes, I actually felt a subtle vibration as I scanned my abdomen. At first, I thought it was gas. Believe me, I had that too. As a girl from a farm, growing up on a solid diet of meat and potatoes, the vegetarian fare we had been eating raged havoc with my digestive system. This new sensation was different, like little bubbles breaking below the surface in a cascade down toward my groin. I resisted the urge to yell out, "Hey guys, I felt something!"

I really like to share things with others! The fact is, I had been feeling things all along, but they were not happening the way that I thought they should be. *When will I learn that expectations create issues for me?* My roommate described the energy as electricity moving through her during a discussion with our teacher within the first few days of the retreat. That is how I imagined the subtle sensations should be. I wanted to keep paying attention to the feeling and enjoy it longer but carried on. We were meant to observe, not react, and whatever we felt would also pass. And it did. That was it. I was back to my typical responses for the rest of the session. During the second group meditation in the hall later in the day, I felt a very brief wave of warmth as I examined my chest but otherwise it was uneventful.

At that point I was getting value from the retreat in the long periods of silence and times outside the hall. In the hours off my cushion I contemplated events in my life. I flashed back to my wedding day and how elated I was to be marrying Stew. We were surrounded by people who loved us, and I was trying to soak up every moment of the day. Easily one of the greatest days of my life and while it was over twenty years ago, I can still recall how I felt, like it was yesterday. It was a buildup of emotion—nerves, excitement, love, anticipation, fun, laughter and the overwhelming need to cry. But I didn't. I stifled the tears, not because I was worried about my mascara running or how red puffy eyes would look in the pictures. My concern was that if I allowed the flood gates to open they wouldn't close. *And what would be so bad about that?* So, I pasted a dazzling smile on my face and disconnected.

There were only a few moments where I let my guard down and shed a tear before I slammed the box around my heart closed. One moment was when my brother Trevor gave me a quick kiss and told me he loved me. The other was listening to my sister-in-law Gail sing at the church. That's it—two moments in an amazing forty-eight-hour period did I allow myself to feel real, genuine emotion.

There I was, surrounded by the expression of unconditional love that I had been craving my whole life, and I put it at arm's length because I didn't know how to accept it. I didn't know how to take it all in! On the happiest day of my life, I didn't feel worthy. I had found the deep line in the rock of my subconscious.

I was hiding. Hiding, in plain sight. Again, something I realized I had been doing for years. I was carrying a suitcase full of emotional baggage, with each item of clothing a layer to cover up the real me. And most of all I was hiding how miserable I felt.

During an evening of visiting and wine drinking I shared with my friend Della that I had low self-esteem. Her response was, "Fuck off. When I met you, I thought you were one of the most confident women I knew." That was all part of the secret that I had never shared, the facade and the image that I worked very hard to create. Every morning I put on a mask of confidence, strength, and an "I've got it all together" demeanor.

There were times when that ability came in handy. Like when I was about to give my first injection to a real live person, my instructor complimented me on my calm and professional mannerism. Or the night I was the pumper operator for my first 911 fire call, and I appeared calm to everyone but my friend Clark to whom I had admitted I was literally shaking in my boots. Both times keeping emotions in check was a good thing. It wasn't those times that created the problem.

Where I was hiding most was those times when I was stressed, scared, unhappy, vulnerable, or angry. Not only did I not know how to express them or process the emotions in a healthy way, I chose to most times keep it to myself. *If you don't have anything nice to say, don't say anything at all.* So, I wasn't saying it out loud, just internally to myself. I became so good at berating and picking myself apart I soon didn't even recognize the good in me. Those mental actions became vocal actions, and finally the physical actions of not taking care of myself physically.

I recognized the physical actions as disciplines or habits that I had created in my life. Because of the mental mess I had going on, it was far easier to stay in a cycle of unhealthy or detrimental habits. I remembered an exercise I had done at Breakthrough to Success where we were asked to follow rules of participation and later in the week when we were asked if we kept those agreements, I was among many that admitted that we had not. The next question was, "When did you know you would break that agreement?" It was one of those exercises that showed me I was constantly making commitments to myself to exercise, to eat healthy, to get organized or to reach some goal, and when I didn't follow through on the actions, my inner bully would say, *"See told you so. You're not worth the effort it takes, you can't do this."* It was so much easier to cling to those unhealthy thoughts, beliefs, and actions than to create new healthy habits. I had read that we don't keep our agreements for one of three reasons: comfort, approval, or rebellion. I definitely had all three of those going on. If I wanted to make the change to healthy disciplines and loving self-care, it would start with the mental action of loving and appreciating myself, being compassionate, and kicking the bully's ass to the curb. It was time. She had already taken up too much space in my luggage!

Additionally, I had nicely buried the negative emotions, but in the process, I had also hidden the good attributes, in part because it never felt good enough. The striving and achieving to always be better and be perfect created an internal cycle of longing for more. *Here's the craving that is creating my misery.* I had accomplished some pretty amazing things in my life, but that's not what I had been focusing on." Another rule I recognized from childhood was: "Don't brag about how good you are because people won't like you". So, I learned from a young age to not celebrate my successes. It was no wonder that when I went into job interviews, and they asked me about my strengths, I was tongue-tied. I was really great at telling the potential employers my weaknesses but saying nice things about myself made me very uncomfortable. If someone gave me a compliment, I would immediately start in with qualifiers and rationalizations. I didn't know how to receive it graciously. I now understood the effects of that childhood brule: if I don't acknowledge my successes and the good in me internally, I won't like myself. *If I don't like and love myself how do I expect others to?*

In his book *The Sedona Method,* Hale Dwoskin highlights how as adults we suppress our natural exuberance for life. He states, "We become more responsible to others' expectations of us than to the needs of our own emotional well-being." I have always been a talker, which was why it was surprising to those who knew me that I would do a silent retreat, but more than being vocal—I am loud.

One of the childhood rules I remember clearly hearing from my Grandma Audrey was that children should be seen and not heard. I have been "shushed" many times, and while those reprimands may have started as lines drawn in the sand, I believe eventually they started to solidify and become deeper. My siblings told me on several occasions that I have no filter, and that I need to watch what I say.

This tendency combined with my stinky thinking and pushing away my emotions was like the perfect storm for depression. I had learned the Sedona Method as a way of bringing awareness to my feelings, allowing, and then releasing them. This technique, while surprisingly simple, was effective. It gave me permission to have feelings, both good and bad, as well as a step-by-step approach to deal with them in a healthy way, rather than stuffing them away to continuously surface like volcanic eruptions. While I had been off the medication for years, the whole idea of processing emotions was a new experience for me, and it was time to start taking care of my own emotional well-being. In the silence, I mentally stated it was time to let go, and live out loud.

I had done a lot of soul searching that day. I was ambivalent about going into this evenings discourse. I was exhausted and just wanted to crawl in bed, but I went anyway. Goenka didn't disappoint as he shared that the most important truth we must accept is that there is misery and it is universal. We were not just to accept that on an intellectual level but actually observe it objectively. I liked the fact that he is acknowledging the negative part, I always struggled with the idea that if I could do affirmations and think positive the whole world would be sunshine and lollipops. This teaching seemed more real to admit that there are hardships in life, and it is how we handle them that is important.

The whole group was laughing out loud as Goenka described the significance of sitting for one hour. In half an hour the misery (pain) starts, and then we would manage another fifteen minutes before the real torture started. He shared that many students came to him and said, "Goenka, I like it very much, the path is good, the discourse is good, but please take out one hour sitting—everything else is so wonderful."

He continued, "I would also like to take it out, but it doesn't work. You have to face." His description was so accurate, and it was nice to hear him verbalize it for all of us. After forty-five minutes every minute felt more like an hour. I burst out again when he described wanting to open our eyes to check our watches because an hour had passed, and we thought the teacher had forgotten to give the signal. *That was totally me in the first four days, except I forgot my watch, so the Universe was trying to help me!* When I heard the chanting, I was happy because I knew that it was almost over. True to form, Goenka sensed my thoughts. With that twinkle in his eye, he said, "The chanting is so enchanting because you know you will soon be out of the bondage of misery." And that was what I was here to experience— learning to come out of the restrictions of unhappiness that had held me captive. The limits that I had created for myself.

Vipassana was meant to be a practice of how to face our daily lives. If I could remain equanimous and not react when things were going well then it prepared me for those times when I needed more strength and resilience to get through. If I could learn to observe it objectively and acknowledge it, then it would pass much quicker. He used the example of physical pain, that it is only intensified when we react to it, creating an aversion. If we just notice it and allow it, we recognize that it will pass. Putting more attention on it, complaining and obsessing about it, is reacting. Encouragement was given to keep practicing objectivity. Our guru shared that the impurities of the mind were sleeping volcanoes. The pressure keeps building unless the root causes are taken out permanently. If we don't attend to those root causes, eventually a volcanic eruption occurs, and one is over taken by negativity.

For so many years, I thought the way to deal with emotional pain was to ignore it, push it away, and pretend it wasn't there. The pain kept growing, repeating, intensifying, and building until I could no longer push it away. If I had allowed it to surface, and acknowledged what I was feeling, it would have passed. Instead, years of resisting had led to even more pain and unhappiness. One of the Success Principles was what we resist persists. Things might have been different if I had let go—lived authentically instead of trying to hide the real me. Since I process things through talking and writing—that would be an excellent way to make it objective. So, the emotions of the heart and the thoughts of the head are so connected. Cool!

I drifted back to the room and Goenka's voice to hear him say that the first noble truth is the fact of suffering. The second is to go deeper and find that the origin of misery is internal not external. *If I am looking for appreciation, acknowledgment, love and happiness from outside, I will be let down and constantly searching for it. I create a craving.* He pointed out that we keep on using our strength and attention to rectify the outside. He reminded us that we cannot change others. When unwanted things happen, we must look for the cause of our misery inside. If I wanted to be happy it would have to be from the inside out, not expecting it to come when all was right and good in the outside world.

Focusing on wanting others to be a certain way or do particular things would not be the path to happiness. If I am the only one who can change me, I can't expect to change others. I can't control them, and I can't change them but what I can do is accept them where they are at, ask for what I need, and realize that they are not responsible for my happiness—I am. Just like they are responsible for their own happiness. I flashed back to wanting to protect Mom and Dad from pain after Dale's death and realized that it didn't matter what I did or didn't do I could not be responsible for their emotional well-being. That went for everyone I loved, including Stewart and the kids. I couldn't make them happy, but what I could do was be a role model of happiness. By being on this path, I was not only helping myself I could empower others.

Expanding on the noble truth that the cause of the misery is on the inside, he again referred to the *saṅkhāra*—we create a craving or an aversion. Goenka described attachments as beliefs and things that are mine. I interpreted this as self-image, how I saw myself compared to how others saw me. If somebody said something hurtful to me, it is not what they say that causes my pain it is what I say to myself or how I interpret their message that becomes important. My reaction to the words or actions is my point of power.

Memories of silly things that I let bother me kept popping up. Stew and I were on our way to his company Christmas party. It was a black-tie affair, and I had spent hours in the salon having my hair done. I was so excited because my whole life I had short hair and had grown it out so I could have an elegant up-do. I tried to act casual when I asked him what he thought of my hair. His honesty wasn't really what I wanted to hear. I wanted him to tell me how sophisticated and beautiful I looked. Instead he looked it over and asked me if I was trying to look ten years older. Ouch, that hurt. Obviously, he had not received the memo that said: say nice things to your wife because she has a fragile ego. I immediately sulked, and then later that night retaliated by telling his colleagues of his faux pas. The truth is I probably did look ten years older, but I had a great time that night trying to prove I was many years younger. *In reality, I pouted like a ten-year-old girl.* Instead of focusing on how I felt—glamorous and elegant—it was lost when I looked for approval from outside.

To illustrate attachment to "mine," Goenka told a story of receiving a beautiful and expensive watch from a friend. When it fell and broke, he was very upset and cried at the loss of his treasured belonging. When another friend broke his expensive watch, Goenka was not at all upset, as he had no attachment to his friend's beloved trinket. I thought of the belongings in my life, and at times how I had surrounded myself with more and more stuff, much of which I didn't need. The last attachment Goenka referred to made me sit up and take notice because this was one area that I had been really examining—the attachment to my beliefs, traditions, rites, and rituals.

It reminded me of the story of a little girl watching her mother prepare ham for Easter dinner. When the girl asked why she cut the end off the meat, the mother replied that she didn't know and called her mom to ask. The reply always made me laugh. The grandma simply said, "Because it never fit in my roasting pan." I thought of how I had learned to cook and sew from my mom. For many years I did try to emulate her, but it wasn't until I started challenging long held traditions, ideas, and really discovering what and who I wanted to be, that I realized I didn't enjoy being domesticated. In fact, I had a pretty strong aversion to it. I smiled to myself because that was one realization that wouldn't be welcome when I returned home from the retreat.

I was five days away from heading home; I still had discoveries to make and knowledge to learn from Goenka. He continued on with the evening discourse to explain that each time we had a craving or an aversion, it created a sensation in our body. Wisdom came when we recognized this was not permanent and need not react. The guru cautioned while it was easy to understand at the intellectual level, experiencing it would be most important. He concluded by saying when we stop generating new sankharas the old ones will come up from the deepest level—as some sensation or another. And then they would pass away. Arising and passing away. Goenka assured us that the path was one of ten thousand steps, and as long as we took one step at a time we were moving toward real peace, real happiness, and real harmony.

For now, my one step needed to take me to bed as the exhaustion I felt before the discourse had returned, and I was ready to drift quickly to sleep.

Simple Steps to Reignite Your Compassion

Stir Your Soul | Accept others where they're at, ask for what you need, and realize that others aren't responsible for your happiness.

Power Up Your Potential | If you want to make the change to healthy disciplines and loving self-care, start with loving and appreciating yourself. Acceptance, appreciation and love begin on the inside.

Activate Your Awareness | Become aware of how you communicate with yourself inside your head. Notice any unkindness and change it to a compassionate and self-loving statement or question.

Rock Your Resilience | When undertaking any goal, remember that beginnings are exciting, middles can be a challenge, and the end is always worth it.

Kick Ass With Intentional Action | Look at yourself in the mirror—truly look—without judgement. Tell yourself something wonderful about you that you really appreciate.

Day Six

"Trauma is personal. It does not disappear if it is not validated. When it is ignored or invalidated the silent screams continue internally heard only by the one held captive. When someone enters the pain and hears the screams healing can begin."

Danielle Bernock, Emerging with Wings: A True Story of Lies, Pain, and the Love That Heals

"When I really looked at them, the actual events didn't hold significance, it was the meaning that I attached to them. I thought of times I had been hurt by something someone said and realized it wasn't their words or even them that hurt me. It was what I said to myself that mattered."

Day 6

Reignite Your Joy

I was on the downward slope of the hill. I made the halfway mark, and while the days felt like they were getting longer, the number of days left was on the decline. My first thoughts of the morning were filled with apprehension, as I worried that as the end drew near I wasn't sure I was making progress. I had felt sensations and in the evening discourses Goenka spoke of not searching—if it is there, it's there; if not, move on. He also stressed that experiencing the sensations was most important, not just understanding Vipassana intellectually. I felt like I needed more reassurance, so I planned to speak with the assistant teacher, Sharon, at lunch.

Remembering Goenka's comment that on the sixth day the students start to work diligently, nudged me out of bed. I dragged myself to the meditation hall by 4:40 a.m. I smiled as I thought of how easy I popped out of bed on the first mornings. I was making my comfort more important and feeling rebellious. Yet, if I was really honest with myself, resistance was playing its hand. Over the last few days, I had been allowing experiences and memories to float into my consciousness. At earlier times in my life, I usually ignored them or pushed them away and when I really looked at them, the actual events didn't hold significance, it was the meaning that I attached to them. I thought of times I had been hurt by something someone said and realized it wasn't their words or even them that hurt me, it was what I said to myself that mattered.

The stories I created in my head were the cause of my misery. This exploration was providing plot twists in the way I had viewed my life movie, and sometimes I looked more like the villain than the heroine. This morning I was willing to take another peek, and I surprised myself by lasting seventy minutes before returning to the warmth of my bed and a quick nap before breakfast.

As I entered the dining hall, I became aware that I felt trapped, and for the first time since arriving, I felt like a captive. I had gone to the manager and requested to get in my vehicle, so I could get more toothpaste—I had run out. Rather than giving me the keys and letting me go, she told me that they would find me some. At the time I thought it was strange that I couldn't quickly grab something from the parking lot, but as I look back they probably thought I was going to bolt if I took possession of my keys. Even walking outside that morning didn't soothe my feelings of restriction and confinement. The rope around the perimeter may have been a six-foot fence with barbed wire at the top. I couldn't shake the restlessness. I couldn't put my finger on exactly what was causing it.

Even when I sat on my meditation cushion, I felt tension. I was trying so hard to make something happen. I imagined I looked like one of those cartoons when the characters are working hard, and the smoke is coming out their ears. Not that anyone would see that because we were sitting with eyes closed. I continued with my scans from the top of my head to the toes as we were directed to do. Then I moved my awareness back up my body. I loved how Goenka said very staccato: *top-of-the-head-to-tip-of-the-toes-tip-of-the-toes-to-top-of-the-head.* He repeated it several times at the beginning of the meditation and even now when I close my eyes can bring back that memory and smile. Yet that morning, I struggled through the meditation, which solidified my resolve to talk to Sharon.

Meeting with the assistant teacher did help my mood considerably. I confessed to her that I had been feeling frustrated with my progress and that I believed I had developed a craving for sensation. From the teachings, we had learned these cravings were what caused the misery in our lives. I was creating the very thing I was here to learn about not doing.

"I'm frustrated with myself, doubting that I am going to feel the subtle sensations," I explained. "I've had struggles with meditation in the past and I have this tendency to put pressure on myself about doing things right."

Sharon smiled her warm, maternal smile, and in her soft voice said, "Carla, you're doing everything exactly right. Everything you are feeling is normal. Just relax and enjoy the process."

That's easy for her to say she probably hasn't been pushing away feelings her whole life. It took me years to get good at that.

"But when I relax, I fall asleep. I'm not sleeping well at night."

"With meditation, we actually need less sleep," she shared. "When you can't sleep at night do Anapana for a time."

It was definitely nice to hear I was having the standard response, but it dawned on me I was again searching for external feedback and had fallen back to my habit of not relaxing into the experience or letting things happen and unfold naturally.

"Through the years there had been many tests of the best length of time for the Vipassana retreat. They determined that seven days was too short, and you will soon see why," she explained.

She made it sound so mysterious as though she had a crystal ball and could see into the future. She obviously knew something I didn't.

After speaking with her, there was a shift in my energy and I went into the afternoon session much calmer and ready to accept the reality of whatever came up was meant to come up. I relaxed and settled in. On about the third round of scanning, I felt a sensation as though someone was pouring warm syrup over my head, and it was slowly running down the back of my neck. I smiled to myself and realized that relaxing into it was exactly what I needed to do.

Throughout the meditation, I did have some success with subtle sensations and enjoyed the thought that maybe I was getting this after all.

In the time between our afternoon and evening group work in the hall, I decided to do a walking "meditation" in the yard. The sun was shining brightly and had enough warmth to bring the temperature to a balmy minus fifteen degrees Celsius. As I trudged along the path, the word "control" kept churning in my mind. I had been trying so hard to manage my results and to want to have things in a certain way that met my expectations, I wasn't in the present moment. My desire to be in charge started at a young age when I had experienced in more than one way that life could change or end in an instant. I took the weight of the world on my shoulders and believed that being strong meant being in command. The sensation I got from trying to control my emotions, my surroundings, my unhealthy eating, my "right" choices and sometimes other people—was a craving. Cravings created misery. I also had an aversion to not having control and both of these were creating stress in my life.

I stopped in my tracks, took a deep breath, and with my eyes closed, raised my face to feel the light and heat from the sun on me. In that moment I thought if I could release myself from expectations and accept things as they are rather than as I thought they should be I would feel free. And calm. And happy. My attention had been focused on feeling the sensations that I missed the whole point to just observe what is and not react. As Goenka had said, remain equanimous.

I returned from my walk and made my way to the kitchen for evening tea. Once in my place I started retracing my earlier thoughts about stories I created. It was clear one of the common themes was judgment. I had very rigid ideas about what was right and wrong based on ideas and experiences from my life. These could be related to the cravings and aversions that Goenka kept referring to. Growing up in a small town I was aware that not only did everyone know your business they also had an opinion about it. Being unique, different, or unusual was certainly not encouraged. I'm not really sure if that was the environment or the era, but it certainly helped shape some of my beliefs and actions. I easily fell into the same pattern and any choice that was different from one I would make was judged as wrong. Prior to the retreat this was one of the thought patterns I had been changing. Placing my judgement on someone else said more about me as a person than it did about them. Appreciation and acceptance of others, their beliefs and actions had actually started making me feel better.

I used to joke that I wanted to be the first to arrive and the last to leave a party; otherwise I might be the focus of the gossip and discussion. I'm not proud that I had often participated in these sessions. Talking about others' faults, scandals and dramas was really just a way to avoid looking at my own. But in many ways, I judged myself harder than anyone else ever could.

I had always been very rule-bound, and if I broke a rule, even self-imposed ones, my inner bully got to celebrate as I was filled with guilt and shame—both emotions that contributed to the negative spiral I had been in. The lessons I learned in this retreat were meant to help me with the reconciliation of judgement, guilt, and shame. I could adopt the mantra, "It's not wrong or right, it just is." I had that profound awareness as the gong rang for us to return to the meditation hall.

During the last sit of strong determination that day, I relaxed into it more so than I had been doing. I thought I would experiment with this realization that I didn't need to control my outcome, I just needed to be an observer and see what came up. The recording of Goenka's message to work patiently, work diligently, and work ardently was followed by his chanting which marked the beginning of the meditation. *Relax, top of the head, face, shoulder, arm. There's a flow of sensation there. Chest nothing, abdomen—there are the bubbles. Back, hips, legs, toes.* Back up now. *Twinge in my calf muscle, ache in my hip. Just breathe.* I carried on, moving my attention up and down as I had been instructed.

BAM! Holy shit!

I had my attention on my right arm when suddenly pain erupted on the left side of my chest. Not a twinge or pressure but a sharp intense pain that came on so fast it literally knocked my body back against the wall and I lost my breath for a moment. It felt like somebody had hit me with a baseball bat and crushed my ribs. I was tempted to open my eyes and see if there was someone who had kicked me. *OK, this is just pain. It will pass. Breathe. I can do this. Breathe. Go back to scanning the arm. I am observing not reacting, BREATHE. Scan the arm. Crap, it's getting worse. I can hardly take a deep breath. OK, maybe shift positions.* As I squirmed, a sudden rush of heat came over my entire body. If I had a mirror and I was able to open my eyes, I expected my face would be flushed. It was as though I had spiked a very high temperature in a matter of minutes. I hadn't yet had menopause hot flashes but wondered if I just had my first. I didn't think the pain could get worse from the initial blast, but it intensified along with the heat. I had to get cool or I was going to faint. *This is what I wanted—some sign. Apparently, I need to be careful what I wish for.*

All thoughts of trying to be equanimous and be objective were lost while I shimmied the blanket loose from my shoulders. I was in survival mode, under attack from my body. Trickles of sweat rolled down the small of my back, my skin was on fire, and I felt light headed. *I'll just take my sweater off. Breathe. Why isn't this fucking pain passing? It's getting worse.* Then the first twinges in the glands at the base of my jaw arose. Saliva built in the back of my throat. *I'm going to throw up!! Not here, I have to get out of here.* I popped my right eye open and looked at the assistant teacher. Nothing. She sat meditating with a serene look on her face. I thought my moving around had generated enough noise that she might be watching me, and I could indicate to her that I needed to break the rules and leave to be sick. *Screw the rules! I am creating a disturbance. Better to ask for forgiveness than permission.* I launched myself up, slapped my hand over my mouth and bolted up the stairs. I was pretty sure I tripped over someone's foot on my way out, but never looked back. I barely made it to the toilet at the top of the stairs before vomiting.

Five minutes or so later, I stumbled out of the bathroom like a limp noodle. I had very little strength. The flushing and heat were gone, but the pain remained and had only diminished slightly. As I opened the door, the manager Melanie was there with a look of concern.

With my throat raw from vomiting, I croaked, "Pain in my chest."

As she helped me to my room, a second staff member had been sent by Sharon to check on us and with few words, Melanie assured her she could return to the hall—she had it handled. *I'm glad she thinks it's handled, cause I'm not so sure.* I laid on my bed for mere seconds before the next wave of nausea hit me like a truck. It must have come with a shot of adrenaline because minutes before I hardly had the strength to move, and yet I was able to get to my bathroom in time to be violently ill again. I threw up so hard I peed my pants.

And then it was over. Just as suddenly as it had come, the pain was gone.

"It may not feel like it right now, but this is really good 'cause you just released some deep shit," Melanie reassured me.

As bizarre as it might seem, I felt great at that moment. I felt light and euphoric. I sensed something had shifted in me. I had no intellectual knowledge of the *saṅkhāra* I had released, but I had no doubt that was what I had experienced. During my talk with Melanie I asked if this kind of response was common. She shared a story of her own physical reaction during a retreat years ago. I recalled before I came to the retreat that someone said our subconscious mind was there to protect us and asked me why I would want to delve into it. At the time I couldn't answer them. After what I had gone through, I believed that I had a deep wound buried in my memories that needed to be released. Protection from the subconscious mind is important, but I also see how it has held me back from really being happy. Those deep negative thoughts and beliefs were stuck waiting to resurface. I just didn't know what was stuck. As I made my way down to the meditation hall for the evening discourse, I decided to let go of the need to know. I chose to observe and be equanimous.

I had agreed to sit in a chair at the bottom of the stairs in order to facilitate a quick and less disruptive exit should the need arise. When we entered the hall again, there was the chair with a bucket under it and Melanie handed me a cold cloth as I sat in my temporary spot. *This is unnecessary I feel perfectly fine.* I felt like I was floating. I was elated that something big had happened for me. I smiled as it struck me I was getting special treatment—the VIP service—for Vipassana Induced Puking! Yet even with what had just occurred, I was able to pay attention to what was being said in the evening session. Goenka congratulated the group having crossed another hurdle because the second day and the sixth day were both very big days in Vipassana. I felt very empowered when he told us it is difficult for a weak-minded person to pass this hurdle. His analogy at the beginning of the retreat was that we were doing a surgery and on the second day many felt like running away. On the fifth day the operation went even deeper and the discourse discussed the reality that there is so much misery in life. Our teacher shared that many people feel that this is too pessimistic, and they try to find excuses to leave on the sixth day. *That must have been what I couldn't put my finger on—the restricted and confined feeling was part of the natural progression.*

It seemed as though every night the evening discourse was exactly what I needed to hear. Goenka spoke in more detail about cravings and losing the balance of our mind when we want something on the outside. I thought of objects I had wanted like a beautiful home, a new vehicle, or travel to exotic locations. Many things I already owned, and yet when I had them, there was always something more to obtain or want. Goenka referred to it as the bottomless bucket, always wanting, more thinking that we would be happy when we got it. His words startled me as he spoke of the craving as an addiction. His example of alcohol addiction intrigued me when he said it is not the substance itself rather the sensation we get from it that is the craving. When I first arrived at the retreat and had talked with Rochelle, she shared that her addiction was education. She kept getting degrees and taking courses to prove herself to others. I immediately thought of my main addiction—food.

My compulsive eating started when I was a teenager in the aftermath of my brother's death. I remember coming home from school and searching the cupboards and eating whatever I could get my hands on. I ate from the time I got off the school bus until supper, ate with the family, and then snacked until bedtime. It was as though I was empty and even when my stomach ached from being stuffed with food, I still longed for more. I didn't recognize that I was using food as my drug. I didn't know how to nurture myself in any other way. I had used food to cope my whole life, check out mentally, and eat to fill the void. The sensation I longed for was love and acceptance. It was a vicious cycle. I ate to feel loved, and when I ate, my inner bully chastised me for eating too much, or for eating unhealthy when I obviously knew better. *Not much love and acceptance there!* Deep down, food became both a source of emotional nourishment and a way of punishing myself because I berated myself when I didn't show proper control and will power over it. On that night as I sat and listened to the discourse and the words of my teacher, I had clarity, and with that came the hope that I could start to choose better for myself. Part of the message that night was that there is a way to come out of misery and that way was to start observing the sensations.

Goenka reassured the group that we stopped generating new *saṅkhāras* when we observed sensations but did not react to them. The old ones from the past would come to the surface and pass away. *I think that's what I witnessed today only I wouldn't call it passing away I would refer to it more as a purge!* It felt like Goenka was looking right at me when he said, "No one else can do this for you. Only you can do the work, only you can eradicate them." *I guess that makes sense. I am the one who has created these thoughts and beliefs and it will be up to me to resolve them.* It felt somewhat reassuring when the teacher started talking about the enemies of meditation. This gave me confidence that I was not alone in my struggle, that others didn't find this process a piece of cake like I might have thought.

In fact, I had met and become familiar with all the obstacles that were being outlined in the discourse. Craving a certain sensation was something I had discussed in my meeting with Sharon. I had also created an aversion to having sensations like pain when what I expected were subtle flows of energy. The third foe was physical sluggishness and mental torpor. I interpreted this as being drowsy and lethargic, both of which I had experienced. The fourth hindrance described was agitation and worry. *Boy I had that one nearly the whole time I've been here.* Doubt and uncertainty rounded out the list of hurdles that made this process a challenge. And I had mastered both of those nicely. While these were being associated with meditation, I noticed that they could also be applied to life in general.

We were encouraged to keep on working so we could come out of our misery. Before coming to the retreat, I had still worried occasionally about having to go back on anti-depressants, but I felt like now I had the antidote to it. I was comforted when Goenka shared that the final goal was to be full of love and compassion, to stop harming myself and others. I moved one step closer to connecting to the happiness I longed for. As the discourse drew to a close I reflected again that I had cleared something earlier in the day that was important, and it had caused a shift in me. I knew I wanted to experience life differently than I had been.

As I started to make my way to my room, Melanie approached me, "Do you need anything?" I shook my head. "Let me know if anything happens in the night and be sure to report to me in the morning."

"I'm fine," I assured her.

"Most people would be running if they went through what you went through today," she shared.

This is exactly what I wanted to happen— something dramatic!

It was also not lost on me that in the past few hours I had been allowed to talk with the manager and the assistant teacher. In a ten-day silent meditation retreat, I had found a way to talk. *Interesting. Did I manifest this?* It was something I pondered as I prepared to go to bed.

When I finally closed my eyes, I had yet one more interesting experience happen to close out the very full day. Generally, when I had closed my eyes for meditation or to visualize I didn't see actual images or anything at all, just like a black screen. That night as I closed my eyes I had the most vivid picture of blue and purple shapes moving fluidly in my mind. *I wonder if this is what having a hallucination is like? What the heck did I clear today?* I felt peaceful and relaxed as I easily dropped off to sleep minutes after crawling into bed.

Simple Steps to Reignite Your Joy

Stir Your Soul | Consider that every emotional hurt you're carrying around with you is connected to a story you've told yourself.

Power Up Your Potential | The stories you create in your head are the cause of your misery, or your peace. Create stories that bring you peace.

Activate Your Awareness | Realize that it's what you say to yourself that really matters, not the actual event or what someone else says or does.

Rock Your Resilience | Let go of the need to control—your emotions, your surroundings, other people. This is a craving which causes misery.

Kick Ass With Intentional Action | Recall an event that caused you to feel embarrassment or guilt and create a new humourous story around the event.

Day Seven

"Owning our story can be hard but not nearly
as difficult as spending our lives running from it.
Embracing our vulnerabilities is risky but not nearly as
dangerous as giving up on love and belonging and joy
—the experiences that make us the most vulnerable.
Only when we are brave enough to explore the darkness
will we discover the infinite power of our light."

Brené Brown

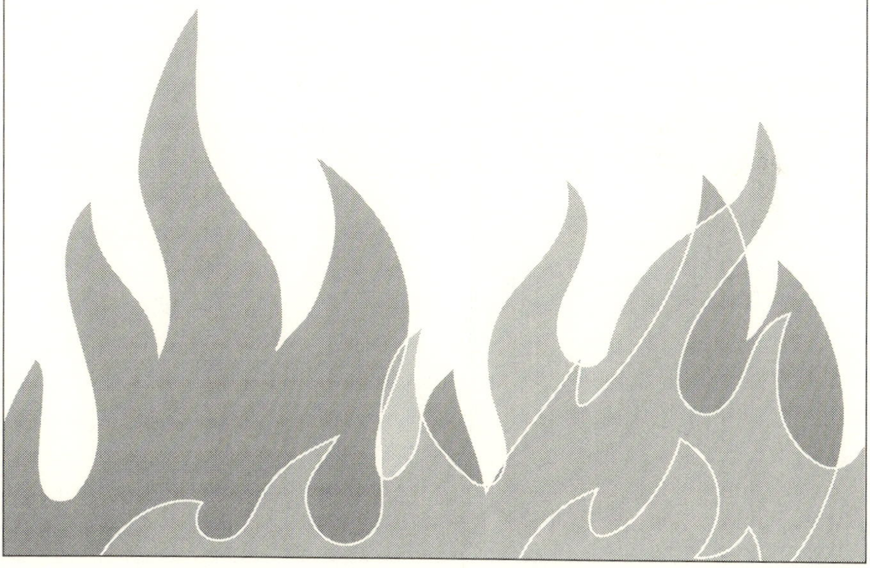

"I realized that I had allowed myself to release some longheld sadness, and I felt one step closer to the happiness I came to find."

Day 7

Reignite Your Self-Care

My Grandma Jean used to say that she "slept like I died." Fortunately, I hadn't died, but for the first time since I had arrived at the retreat I had a terrific sleep. The last time I had seen the clock it read 9:45 p.m. and when I opened my eyes at 4:05 a.m., I was surprised and relieved. The events of the previous afternoon clearly had shifted something in me. I had agreed to check in with Melanie to let her know how I was feeling so I climbed out of bed and got dressed. As my eyes adjusted to the lights in the bathroom, the reflection in the mirror caught my attention. I noticed that I looked refreshed and my eyes were shining. I felt like I had a split personality, on one hand feeling alert and fresh and on the other feeling drained. It was a different fatigue than I had been experiencing from the lack of sleep, and I recognized it more as tiredness from hard work.

I brushed my teeth and ran a brush through my hair. Even though I had full intentions to go back to bed, I made the effort to get dressed and do some basic morning care rather than meet with the manager in my pajamas accompanied by crazy bed head and morning breath. Granted it was part of my routine, but in reality, there was still a part of me that cared about being judged. *What judgement would she make, that I'm an ugly sleeper who doesn't wake up perfectly primped and polished? Wow, there are some deep insecurities about my looks and how others see me. If I showed up and didn't take the time to do my hair or do basic self-care people might think I was lazy, have no self-respect, or even worse they might figure out I'm not perfect. Or... they might think I'm normal.* I smiled at a childhood memory of my mom coming in from the yard, washing up, running a comb through her hair, and putting on lipstick so she could go to town for something. Obviously, my beliefs about personal grooming and image started at a very young age, as did many of the other rules, roles and expectations that I had been carrying around with me. Many of those had surfaced and been released or rejected both before and during the retreat.

The lights in the common area felt bright and intrusive as I left the darkness of my bedroom to find Melanie and report my status. I didn't see anyone in the hallway or dining area. It was too early for anyone to be heading to the meditation hall. I paused momentarily at the top of the stairs and noticed the quiet and the stillness of the house. Even though this was a silent retreat, when people were present there was still noise and movement. I had a fleeting thought that I needed to have more of those stop, look, and listen moments where I noticed the space between chaos or activity, and took time for serenity. Instead of staying with that idea, I carried on, as I usually did when I was on a mission. I headed toward the kitchen and just before I reached the door to knock, Melanie came out carrying a cup of tea.

She gave me a quick smile, "How are you?"

I responded quickly to say, "I'm fine. I had a great night sleep, but I want to go back to bed for a while."

Her pointed response of, "That's great. Have a nice rest," felt like validation that it was acceptable to miss the early morning meditation time. The exchange was direct and brief, but the talking I had been doing as a result of the experience on day six made me long for more. I resisted the urge to have a more in-depth conversation with her. Instead, I smiled and slowly walked up the stairs to my dark, cozy space and climbed back into bed. The morning before, I worried that I was resisting the process when I stayed in bed, but as the seventh day dawned, I recognized that I was giving myself a moment for recovery before I entered the meditation realm again. This awareness was new, and I was comforted that I was honouring my needs. I easily drifted back asleep until I was roused by the breakfast gong and the routine of the day started again.

As the retreat participants drifted toward the kitchen from their respective rooms, I had a flash of zombies moving in slow motion. Something about how we all moved around each other seemed like we were on autopilot and that morning it amused me. To match my jovial mood, I was feeling the need for lighter food so I passed on the oatmeal and chose fresh fruit and toast. Usually, I would consider the hot breakfast a comfort food and dig in to soothe myself, but I was pleasantly surprised that I chose food based on nourishment rather than an emotional bandage.

Instead of lingering in the dining room after breakfast, I returned to my room for a hot steamy soak. I had the strong need to nurture and care for myself. In the tub I scanned my mind to see if any significant memory had surfaced as a result of the very physical reaction, but nothing came immediately, and I closed my eyes to relax. The day before had taken a lot out of me, and I was reeling from the impact of such a noticeable release. I was surprised at how easily I let go of the need to know what caused me to be physically sick. My long-held pattern of analyzing and trying to stay in my head had been replaced with a moment of intuition that what I had released was now less important than how I would respond to the experience. And my response was surprising. I was in caregiver mode, but instead of directing the nurturing and love to someone else, I was giving it to myself.

My friend Trisha once shared that when she was doing a guided meditation she saw me as Mother Earth. I was honoured but confused. I didn't see myself as being the loving, wholesome, and giving spirit that was my version of the epitome of motherhood.

As I sat in the tub and that memory came back to me, tears warmed my cheeks as I recognized that I had not lived my vision of exceptional mothering with Sianna, Rylee, and Shaelyn. Not only that, for years I had denied my own mothering and self-care. In Cheryl Richardson's *Extreme Self-Care* program, she acknowledges, "When we get quiet we allow the feelings to come up and sometimes the first ones to come up are sadness."

Crying softly, I allowed the sadness to come up and be released in my tears. I thought of how I had gradually and almost completely detached myself emotionally first from myself, then in my relationships with others, but most sadly from my children. This was not a legacy I wanted for my kids. The regret formed as an ache in my chest. I spent so much time focusing on poopy diapers, never-ending cleaning, the mountains of laundry and cooking for demanding food critics that I lost sight of the joy and love that they had for life and for me. I abandoned them emotionally when I shut myself off. I cried harder when I realized I had rejected my children just as I had felt rejected myself as a child.

My mom did the same thing after my brother Dale died. From the moment of my brother's death, I watched as my mother slowly isolated herself emotionally. When I look back, I understand the total grief and devastation that she must have felt losing a child. What I saw was that she became detached as the only way she knew how to cope. For years, she went through the motions of life. I now believe that she was clinically depressed, but never received treatment or reached out for support. She did what she could to hide her pain from all of us.

I remember Mom and Dad both returning to their daily activities and work mere days after the tragic accident. I believe they felt this is what they had to do to hold it together and move forward for the rest of us four kids. Staying busy was also the only form of therapy they knew. This grit, determination, and what I then saw as strength was what they had learned from their own parents. It was pure survival instinct, but it also didn't give them the time they needed to heal the deep wound of sorrow. I became aware of another brule—bullshit rules we learn as kids that do not continue to serve us. *Even in the face of crisis if I just keep moving forward, get back to work, and stay busy I can get through it.* That was one of my ways to disconnect.

I witnessed both my parents do the best they could. At first there were a few attempts to talk about feelings, but I was very resistant to share anything with any of the adults. As time passed, I think we all just "carried on" and pushed the feelings further away. I have heard the saying, "Time heals all wounds." *What a load of crap. It's not time that helps.* By simply pushing the sadness, the despair, and the anger away, it festered within my subconscious mind and manifested in different ways.

Since I had come off the antidepressants, my experience was showing me that healing came from allowing the feelings and expressing or releasing them in a safe, healthy way. My emotions had been giving me valuable information, and when I finally started to pay attention, I was able to recognize how they impacted my beliefs and actions.

I started to see patterns in my life. I went from having emotionally unavailable parents to choosing and marrying a man who was also not open with his emotions. He too hid them deep inside. When we went for pre-marriage sessions with the priest, he informed us that the forms we filled out indicated Stew was a thinker and I was a feeler. I didn't want to be the feeler, which felt weaker and less important. I wanted to be an equal partner, strong and powerful. Through the years Stew and I had some serious power struggles while I tried to figure it out.

My definitions of strength and power were formed around my observations of my dad. Up until the death of my brother, I had never seen him cry. I witnessed him momentarily let out a sob as they lowered Dale's casket into the grave and quickly snap back into composure. I equated showing deep emotion as a break in the armor and a loss of that coveted control.

My pattern had been to disregard my feelings and stuff them down. My life was like the cooker my mom used to can vegetables. The pressure would build up inside the pot, and when the force was too great a little bobble sitting on the top would rock back and forth. That was how she knew when to take it off the heat, letting the pressure dissipate so the pot didn't explode. I swallowed sadness, anger, resentment, guilt, hurt, and frustration. Each time any negative or unpleasant feelings would rise to the surface and the pressure would build, I would sense it there, but I would move away to let it dissipate rather than allow and release it.

Like pushing a beach ball under water, when I let go of the tightly held control it popped back to the surface. Or something else would happen to trigger me. Eventually I would explode. The pent-up emotion came out as bursts of anger or sarcastic slams. *But nice girls don't get angry. If you don't have anything nice to say, don't say anything at all.* So, I didn't speak the truth about what I was feeling, and each time I dismissed or dissociated from my feelings, subconsciously I was rejecting a part of who I was.

When I wasn't a raving crazy woman, my attempts at expressing myself turned into a snotty, tear fest. There was so much pent up energy in me I actually experienced physical discomfort when I started to share my feelings at the same time. When I was in a vulnerable situation, a burning pain started in my chest and moved slowly up to my throat where it stopped. It was like someone was choking me, pushing on my neck to stop the release from coming all the way up. An ache built behind my eyes, and only released when I allowed the tears to spill out. Yet, shedding the tears did not relieve the stifling sensation in my throat.

I once had a Reiki session with my sister-in-law, Zina, where I had a moment of letting that energy actually release. When she held her hands near my head and neck, I had this sudden movement internally, like a ball was moving through me from below my belly button all the way up my torso. When it got to my throat, I let out a loud sob. It happened so quickly I didn't have time to stifle it. Suddenly, I was crying as I lay on the massage table. She allowed me time to release what I needed to, and when the session was over I asked, "What the heck was that?" She smiled, looked me directly in the eye and told me, "I was working on your throat chakra and you are not feeling heard. Your voice is not being expressed." I didn't realize it then, but that was just a glance into the work I was doing here at the retreat.

Ignoring the feeler in me totally contradicted my desire to have an intimate relationship with Stew. I had to come to terms first with the fact that I didn't have an intimate relationship with myself, because I was dismissing my feelings as inconsequential. I once read an article that described intimacy as "into me I see." As I was focusing my attention into my inner most thoughts and beliefs, I realized that this would be the first step to connecting with Stew on a deeper level. First, I had to reconnect with me on a deeper level.

Perhaps worst of all, I not only surrounded myself with people I saw as emotionally unavailable, I kept people at arm's length, and in some cases, I had completely shut other people out. When it came to emotions and feelings, I did everything I could to numb them and to push them away. When asked how I was feeling, I couldn't describe it because I had chosen to ignore my feelings.

Emotional detachment became my coping mechanism. It was how I dealt with everything. If I just lived in my head, then everything would be OK. When traumatic things happened, I might cry a little, but quickly regained my composure and dealt with it by eating— smother those feelings with a nice covering of food or by completely putting them on a back shelf in the subconscious mind and keep my mind occupied with mindless TV, hours on Facebook, or surfing the net.

Like my parents, Stew and I had also experienced a traumatic loss, but I had never acknowledged the impact it had on me—not because it wasn't major, but because that was how I had learned to get through crisis.

1996 was baby year. Stew and I had made the decision that was the year that we would have a baby as though you could just enter it in your Day-Timer® or project planning software. I became pregnant quickly, and we were deliriously happy. And as if it really was a project, we were right on schedule for our testing. We had seen the genetics doctors and had ultrasounds all because we knew that Stew carried an inverted chromosome that could be passed on to our baby.

As I lay on the stretcher waiting for the specialist to come in, I had butterflies in my stomach and tightness in my chest. Not because I thought anything was wrong. I was preparing myself for a very long needle to be poked into my bulging belly for the amniocentesis.

The first step in the procedure was to have a routine ultrasound. I observed the darkened room with the only light coming from the computer screen, and wished that I was waiting for someone to come in and give me a massage.

As he entered, Dr. D. seemed really tall from my vantage point on the stretcher. His kind eyes and soft, but professional, voice reassured me. Even though he had done this same procedure hundreds, maybe thousands of times, his bedside manner made me feel like our experience was the only one that mattered. He was so present and so caring. I was expecting the gel to be cold but was pleasantly surprised when it was warm and soothing—adding to my belief that he really cared about my experience. I had a brief moment where I relaxed before the Dr. said "Oh no." Two little words echoed in my mind like a pinball ricocheting in the machine. My voice was like a high-pitched squeal when I asked, "What's wrong?"

I was hearing the words the doctor spoke, and I understood them, but I felt like I was watching a movie, and this was happening to someone else as I looked on. Classic disconnect. Not that I would wish this experience on anyone else, but I sure wished it wasn't happening to us. Dr. D. explained, "The baby has an extremely large cystic hygroma which is a sack of the lymphatic system fluid on the outside of his body. It runs the entire length of his spine. What we see now is a deformity of his head, hands, and feet. It is too early to know for sure, but we would expect there are problems with major organs. With severe anomalies like this, I am surprised that you didn't already have a miscarriage." Within a fifteen-minute procedure, the bubble of excitement, elation, and happiness, we had been living in was popped.

In an instant, our lives changed forever.

There was a flurry of activity that seemed to be happening in slow motion. I was transferred to a wheel chair and taken from the ultrasound area to the procedure room for the amniocentesis. I was so grateful for the chair as my legs were like rubber, and I wasn't sure I had the strength to walk. Stewart hovered quietly beside the wheelchair, holding my hand when he could. I let the tears flow freely, but I held back the sobs that would convulse my body if I allowed them to escape.

Entering this new room, there were no dim lights to create a soothing ambiance. The bright lights and table I climbed up on reminded me of the operating room from nursing school. Several nurses donned in sterile gowns circulated busily preparing for the procedure. When Dr. D. arrived he explained, "I would like to do an additional test called chorionic villus sampling (CVS) when we do the amniocentesis. I will do my best to only poke you once and collect the placental tissue and amniotic fluid at the same time."

I went into analytic mode to question, "Why do you need to do that?"

He replied, "We can get the results quicker with this test, so you can make a decision about what to do with the pregnancy." *What do you mean a decision? Oh my God! They want me to make a choice. Can't they decide for me and tell me what to do.*

Preparations in the cold, sterile room continued. I observed the activity, trying desperately to pretend that I was not completely devastated by the news we had received and that this was a routine medical procedure. "Carla, are you ready?" Dr. D.'s voice pierced my thoughts.

I was lying on my back on a hard table. I glanced down to see my abdomen draped with only a small area of skin showing, now brown from the solution they had used to cleanse the injection site. *When did they put that on?* I completely missed the application of a cold liquid being painted on my body. I closed my eyes and took a deep breath. A woman's soft voice told me to keep breathing, and I focused on moving air in my nose and out my mouth. I heard each expiration as I pushed it through my tight lips. I felt a pinch when the needle first entered. It became a bearable pressure, but I still clenched my toes and hands. After a few minutes I heard Dr. D. say he was sorry he was going to have to poke me twice. I don't think I said anything in response. *I want this to be over. I want to go home. I can't believe this is happening to us. What will we say to people?* The tears that had momentarily stopped now streaked hotly down the side of my face and tickled when they fell into my ears.

The doctor paused before he inserted the second needle and leaned toward my face. "Are the tears because you feel physical pain or are they just emotion?"

Keeping my eyes closed, I nodded.

He said, "Emotion?"

I nodded again. I had opened my mouth to respond to him but couldn't force the words out.

"OK, Carla here we go again," he said compassionately. I never saw his expression, but the kind tone in his voice and taking that brief moment to acknowledge my discomfort touched my heart and the tears fell faster.

We left the clinic completely numb. I had managed to stop crying, but my face was still red and puffy from the tears that I had shed in that short period of time. Stewart was solemn and contemplative. He nearly hit a pedestrian as we drove down the street because he was so distracted and in shock—we both were. I don't remember the conversation during our four-hour drive back home. There wasn't a lot of it as we both sat quietly trying to absorb the information that we had received.

When we arrived home, Stew said he was going for a walk. "Just a minute, let me get my shoes and I'll come with you."

"No, I need to be by myself."

I begrudgingly gave him his space, and I realized much later that we isolated ourselves from grieving together as parents, opting to instead keep our feelings to ourselves. This simple interaction also solidified my learned belief that to be strong and independent you needed to deal with crisis on your own.

The morning after we had returned from Edmonton, Stew and I sat across from each other at the dining room table. We were both sullen, and I was drained from the traumatic day and a fitful sleep. I took a deep breath and asked him, "What do you want to do?" He knew I wasn't asking about his schedule for the day and that it was time to discuss our next move.

He looked across the table and said, "I've got no interest in dealing with a child with this kind of medical issues. We will never have a life of our own. This is not what I want as a parent."

I felt the relief wash over me. I was thinking the same thoughts but was too afraid to say them out loud. I was calm and to the point when I simply said, "I agree."

However, I wasn't sure. Deep down, I felt tremendous guilt for choosing my own needs over the life of this unborn child. It felt selfish to choose an easier life than the one we would be in store for if in fact I was able to carry this baby to term. I experienced even more guilt that the decision was made so quickly and without much deliberation between us at all. Even though I knew this was the right decision for us, I was ashamed to admit to anyone that I was relieved that we had an opportunity to decide the outcome. In a direct and short conversation, we agreed that when we received confirmation of the diagnosis we would terminate the pregnancy—*along with the hopes and dreams we once held for the future.*

The emotion around terminating the life of our baby was difficult to explain to someone who had not been in this situation. We decided to tell our immediate families, and it was painful to watch first the look of shock, then the sadness and their discomfort as they searched for words to comfort us. I felt bad for them because if the roles were reversed, I would want to do or say something to help, and yet I knew there was nothing that would. I recall being quite matter of fact about it, and I recognize now that while it was intensely emotional news to share I was like a talking head, completely separated from my heart and any feelings. We chose to tell those outside of family that I had a miscarriage rather than that we made the decision to terminate the pregnancy. I wasn't prepared to answer questions or talk about it at length. I didn't want to face the judgments of other people because I could barely stand to experience the judgment from myself. I was afraid of letting the flow of sadness, grief, and guilt come out, fearing that it would not stop. It felt too overwhelming to handle. So, I detached and pushed it away.

Because of how far along I was in the pregnancy, I had to go to Edmonton and actually deliver the fetus. The emotional disconnection continued like a crack in the earth, getting wider and deeper. I coped by mentally distracting myself from what was really happening. It all felt surreal. I was admitted to a private room on the labour and delivery floor. Once I had changed into the hospital gown, an orderly arrived with a wheelchair to take me to a treatment room while Stew stayed behind in the room. I paid no attention to the details of my surroundings or the people present in the room. While I had no anesthesia for the procedure, I was numb emotionally, only aware of the uncomfortable stretcher and the physical discomfort when the doctor inserted laminaria tents in my uterus to induce labor. I learned much later that this was actually seaweed that they applied to the cervix to dilate it and begin the process. I was told it was normal to feel the pinching sensation. *Normal, there is nothing normal about any of this. Just get this over with. I want to go home.*

Stew and I passed the hours working on a project. I was in the hospital bed with the gown on, and Stew alternated between sitting in the recliner and the cot they had brought for him to sleep on. I pretended not to notice that the room was equipped as a birthing room where excited parents waited for the delivery of their baby. Sometime during the process, a social worker interrupted our game of "let's ignore the real reason we are here."

She spoke softly when she asked, "What are your plans regarding the fetus?

What the hell do you mean plans? There are no plans. We aren't taking a baby home. That dream is crushed.

We must have looked dumbfounded, so she continued, "Would you like to see or hold the baby?" I was flustered and looked at Stew to respond. Stew spoke directly to the social worker and quietly answered "No." I shook my head to confirm his response, but I wasn't really sure.

OK, good he made the decision for me. If I see the baby or hold the baby that will make this real. I just want this to be a bad dream. I'm afraid to look. I don't want that picture to be burned in my memory.

"Do you want to name the baby and arrange for a memorial or burial?"

Again, Stew responded, "No."

I shook my head. *I don't want to make these decisions. I'm glad Stew is able to speak for both of us.* We both made choices that day. Stew was making the decisions he thought were right for both of us to handle this nightmare, and I gratefully chose to let him be in charge. I often wonder if I had been really present in that moment and connected with my heart, would I have made a different choice? If I had seen him or held him, would I have been able to grieve the loss of my baby and find peace and closure? That was how I had dealt with all difficult things in my life—push it away and not really deal with the deep profound pain of loss.

And then it happened again.

As I had learned to be strong and carry on, we decided to get pregnant again immediately.

Not that another baby could replace the first loss, but it felt like having a baby would somehow help with the healing that our hearts so desperately needed. Again, we went for the testing, and again we were told that the baby had serious life-threatening deformities and anomalies. Now I was pissed off. *God, now you're just being an ass. We already went through this. How could this be happening again? Am I being punished? Is this to teach me some kind of lesson? Well, I don't get it.* This time I wasn't as far along so I was able to have a simplified D & C procedure to terminate the pregnancy. Before going in to the hospital I was instructed by the doctor to say that I was having the procedure for a blighted ovum. Apparently, this was an "acceptable" reason. This did nothing to ease my feelings of shame. In fact, it intensified my fear of judgment and ridicule for a decision that Stewart and I had made.

Sadness was one thing to deal with, but the guilt and shame was something that ate away at me. I didn't want people to know because I was afraid that they would judge me based on their own thoughts and beliefs about what the right thing to do was. It would be years before I was comfortable sharing our story with others, but each time I did, I received pure compassion. As I unburdened my secret, it dissipated the shame. It still pains me greatly to talk about. This was and is a profound and devastating loss in my life. More important than the support I have received from others is the forgiveness and compassion I was learning to give myself. I was taking small steps toward my own self-care—and the retreat was part of that.

The hot steamy bath I had climbed into for nurturing had long ago turned cold, and I realized it was time to haul my pruned skin out and get back to meditating. As I entered the hall for morning sit, I noticed the dining room chair they had for me in the corner the night before was now in place of my comfortable meditation cushions. I felt my body tighten as I reacted and then caught myself and tried to relax. I hadn't been asked if I wanted to continue using the chair, and I had an instant rebellious thought. What felt like VIP service in the evening now felt like I was being coddled. The streak of independence and pride shot through me as I decided I didn't want special treatment now. It was a kind gesture and rather than acknowledging it as such, I immediately went into resistance mode. The psychological walls slammed up around me. In my mind if someone wanted to care for me, I was needy and weak; therefore, I couldn't be the strong woman that I desired to be. I had learned by watching my parents that being strong meant not showing your emotions, quickly jumping back into work after a crisis, detach, and suppress the feelings. Besides, the chair was upright and formal and not nearly as comfortable as my previously established tower of softness. I sat on the chair and resolved to ask for it to be removed before the next session. Out of consideration for the people who had started meditating, I decided I could endure one hour of discomfort.

I took a few deep breaths to center myself and shake off the momentary irritation. The now familiar chanting helped to soothe me as I moved into meditation. There was definitely a bit of trepidation, and a few times I caught myself holding my breath as though if I let myself go there would be a repeat performance from last evening's sit. *Breathe, relax and hang in there. Is it possible that I could have a more traumatic release than I already have? Do I really want to do this? Yes, I do. I feel so good after and this is a way to access the subconscious. Let go of the doubt. Just stay in the present. This is what I came for. Get back to work—this is what I want. Top of the head...* I completed the hour with no significant gross sensations arising, but I was aware that I had only half-heartedly scanned for them. I sensed that I was not yet ready to jump back into deep meditation. Attendance at the group sits were a mandatory part of the experience so I could not opt out just because I needed a rest. Physically, I was in the room, but I chose not to work diligently and ardently as Goenka had instructed. Flashes of a disobedient child came to me as though I was breaking some kind of rule. Then it dawned on me, how would anyone know if I wasn't working hard?

When I met with Sharon after lunch to discuss the removal of the restrictive chair, she took the opportunity to ask how I was coping since I had been physically sick. I paused as I tried to find the words to describe what I was feeling. My response felt silly when I said, "I feel lighter, like a load has been lifted off my shoulders." *More like a load of crap lifted from my subconscious.* Her response surprised me because I thought the reflection I had seen in the mirror that morning was partly in my imagination.

Sharon simply said, "I see a change in you. You look brighter in your face."

I shared with her that at my dad's suggestion I had taken a picture of myself before the retreat and planned to do a post selfie to see if there were noticeable physical changes. She thought that was an excellent idea. As I left the hall to enjoy my free time, I reveled in the idea that the shift I felt internally was reflected on the outside. But I wasn't able to share that revelation with anyone else at the retreat. Sharing with others was how I received affirmations and approval. I recognized it as another craving and that looking externally for it would only cause more misery.

With practice I had been able to move about the house, be in the dining room, and the meditation hall with minimal attention on the other participants. Unlike the first days when I was very focused externally, I had successfully become introspective, so I was surprised by the interaction that happened in the dining room when I returned to the common area following my meeting with Sharon. As I sat on the couch deep in thought I became aware of movement.

Rochelle, my new-found friend from the first day, had been sitting beside me and got up to grab a stool. She placed it right in front of me and turned to get another stool to use as footrests. I didn't look up and catch her eye, but I felt a very deliberate gesture of companionship and smiled to myself. I felt a warm flow of energy wash over me as I interpreted the move as a moment of nurturing and connection. I wondered for a moment whether she was reaching out for her benefit or mine, and either way it was a small action with a huge impact. It was the encouragement that I needed to recognize that even though I was doing this for me. I wasn't in it alone. It was a nice feeling to take into the meditation hall for the afternoon group sits.

When the bell rang, we moved slowly and deliberately down the stairs to the dim sanctuary. There was the usual flurry of activity as everyone settled, plumped pillows, and found their comfort zone. I was happy to see that the chair was removed and once again my cushy spot welcomed me for my hour of meditation. The session was uneventful, as I silently observed for sensations on my body, still a bit wary of what might come up.

I went through the required schedule for the rest of the day and noticed that I felt completely spent. Bed couldn't come soon enough for me. Even my usual enjoyment of the evening discourse was subdued by the awareness that I had earlier in the day.

As I switched the light off, I realized that I had allowed myself to release some long-held sadness, and I felt one step closer to the happiness I came there to find.

Simple Steps to Reignite Your Self-Care

Stir Your Soul | Watch for small gestures of nurturing, companionship and connection and pause to appreciate them when they happen.

Power Up Your Potential | When irritation triggers in your mind, stop and consider where the trigger came from - focusing on the internal cause, rather than the external event.

Activate Your Awareness | Become aware of feelings of guilt and shame and forgive yourself for whatever you're carrying. Be as compassionate with yourself as you would be with others.

Rock Your Resilience | When you quiet your mind and become aware of your feelings, often the first emotion to come up is sadness. Acknowledge it, allow it to flow through you, and it will release more easily.

Kick Ass With Intentional Action | Once again, stand in front of a mirror, only this time, tell yourself lovingly, out loud that you forgive yourself for all of your past mistakes.

Day Eight

"As women, we are taught to meet everyone else's needs before we nurture ourselves. And as we are groomed into compliant beings, we come to believe that the people in our lives will anticipate and meet our needs as we do theirs. When this does not happen, we begin to feel we do not have a right to our needs and desires."

Jennifer Louden, The Woman's Comfort Book.

"I wonder what it would be like if I stopped trying to prove myself and did work on my terms?"

Day 8

Reignite Your Soul Care

The awareness of my surroundings came to me slowly as I opened my eyes. Just as I had easily drifted off to sleep the night before, I effortlessly awoke from a sound sleep. I took the time to stretch my whole body, reaching each end of the cot with my arms and legs before flipping on my side to check the clock. I smiled as I saw the time, 3:59 a.m. *What a difference a week makes. I settled in to a routine. I'm sleeping so deeply, and I wake before the morning gong feeling refreshed. When was the last time I slept so well? When was the last time I jumped out of bed at four in the morning, eager to start the day? Oh right, never!*

I intended to get up for meditation in the hall, but I took a few minutes and just stared into the darkness. I heard Veronica turn over on her bed, the cot creaking to disclose the movement. In the adjoining room, I heard a toilet flush and the rush of water as someone started the shower. Despite the sounds, I had a sense of stillness in the house and wondered if that was tranquility in myself being mirrored in my environment. I enjoyed the moment of peace.

When the 4:20 gong sounded, I climbed out of bed, collected my clothes and made my way to the bathroom. I welcomed the warmth of the heated tiles on my feet. I noticed the lights didn't seem as intrusive that morning. So this is what it feels like to wake up on the "right side" of the bed? I quickly did my daily care and left the room for the meditation hall. For the first time in days I would join the group for the early morning sit.

As I descended to the basement and came into our sanctuary, I noticed there were only four other people. On those days when I was absent from the pre-dawn gathering, I had told myself that I was the only one breaking rules and not committing fully. As I settled into my meditation position, I realized the process was about each of us experiencing this retreat in our own way. Attendance during those hours was not mandatory and that morning I happily chose to meditate rather than stay in bed.

I began scanning my body for sensations, working from the top of my head systematically down to my toes. I was pleased that I was noticing both gross feelings of pain, pressure, or itching, as well as subtle flows of vibration in different parts of my body. The span of time between meandering thoughts had grown substantially, and I now was able to go for long periods before I lost my focus. That morning turned out to be my longest meditation in the hall. When I decided I had enough, I quietly got up and exited to the dining area. I looked up at the clock, surprised to see that it was 5:50 a.m. Instead of retreating to my room and sleeping, as I had done before, I decided to wait for breakfast in the common area.

I pulled a stool to the large window and peered out into the black remnants of the night. I smiled as I thought of my friend Wendy saying, "I was up before God." With it still being dark outside and the lights illuminating the house, the window actually worked more like a mirror and I observed my reflection. I was aware that I just looked and didn't move into my usual diatribe about excess weight, blotchy skin, or dark circles under my eyes. I simply noticed and watched. Soon gentle thoughts merged into my consciousness about compassion, care, and nurturing.

Self-care was always something I told myself I was good at. I spared no expense when it came to having my hair and nails done. I booked regular pedicures and occasionally treated myself to a massage. Stewart always referred to these as my maintenance appointments, and I actually liked that he saw them as regular upkeep rather than luxuries. That way he didn't quibble over the cost. But that was all surface-level pampering, and I was starting to understand that I didn't have a clue about how to nurture my soul.

I decided ultimate self-care was much more than working on the exterior image. It reminded me of when I used to clean the house before guests came over. I polished the piano, cleaned the bathroom, and frantically threw the crap that had been lying around into the closest drawer or closet. I may have tricked them into thinking my home was organized and clean, but I knew about the secrets in the closet. I smiled at the memory and said a little prayer of gratitude that I was a recovering perfectionist and had let some of that go. I was less worried about what others thought, but I now realized the real harm was my internal struggle and judgement.

Being able to access and clear our deep-rooted *saṅkhāras* was like spring-cleaning the house—basement, closets and all. Purging and releasing some long-held sadness, guilt, and shame had already started. I gave myself permission to have compassion, and I looked forward to figuring out how to nurture my soul. But that would have to wait as I became aware of others slowly drifting into the dining room just as the breakfast bell rang.

I ate my meal and then decided to lie down in my room. I stretched out on my back and closed my eyes. I heard Veronica come into the room and rustle around before she lay down on her cot. I tuned into the sensations I was experiencing in my body and felt completely relaxed. I don't know how much time had passed when I felt the familiar pain in my side. It was not as strong as the first time, but it still took my breath away at its sudden arrival. I knew that I was going to throw up. I launched myself from my cot and darted past my roommate into the bathroom. Out of the corner of my eye, I saw her whip her head to watch me. I managed to swing the door shut and vomit in private. Just as before, as soon as the expelling ended, the pain was gone. There was less intensity than the first time, but it was still significant. I washed my face, brushed my teeth, and used the supplies to clean up the bathroom. As I left, I glanced at my roommate and our eyes met for a moment before we both looked away. I was amazed at how such a minor gesture made me feel supported.

A cup of the ginger tea soothed my stomach the last time, so I searched the manager out to make the request. I didn't feel the least bit nauseous but felt that the hot drink had been a comfort. I knocked tentatively on the staff bedroom door. Fortunately, Melanie answered. I smiled and whispered, "I had another episode. Could I get some tea?"

She came out of her room and we stood in the hallway. "Do you think it might be a reaction to the food, because we had someone else feel sick too?"

I shook my head, "No, I have had food poisoning and experienced sickness after eating something that didn't agree with me. This feels different. I think I have opened the wound as

Goenka said, and this is my body's way of helping me bring the noxious stuff to the surface."

"You are an equanimous warrior woman," she said, shaking her head in disbelief. A surge of pride welled up and I felt myself stand a little taller and beamed back at her. I liked her affirmation of my strength. "You inspire me. Most people would be running away."

Don't think that hasn't crossed my mind. I simply replied, "thank you," returning to wait in my room for the tea.

The bell for the group meditation rang a few minutes after Melanie brought my brew so I only had time to drink part of it. I followed the other participants, merging from our respective rooms into a single file to go through the door to the hall. Settling quickly, I watched as others took their places.

Sharon always entered last and made her way to the front of the room. I followed her path with my eyes and was surprised when she stopped part way, turned to look in my direction and walked over. She bent down and whispered quietly, "Would you like a chair at the back of the room, just in case?"

I shook my head and more mouthed the words, "I'm fine, thank you." Again, I bristled at the gesture. It wasn't logical, but her concern made me feel like I was being punished and segregated from the group. I silently questioned whether my physical reaction was out of the ordinary at the retreats.

Sharon left my side, took her position at the front and started the tape. The chanting filled the room. I closed my eyes, focused on my breathing and tried to get into the meditation. On day six, when I had returned to the hall after the pain and purging, I was hesitant about examining for sensations. Even though this latest release wasn't as intense, it still impacted my ability to give the technique my full attention. I struggled with the idea that I wasn't working diligently and making best use of my time as Goenka said so many times in the lessons. But I also felt I needed a little space to soothe myself after the response I had. My mentor Kathy and I had often talked of the power of the pause. She explained that in fly-fishing, she learned that deliberate pauses in the back cast, allowed her line to move forward with greater momentum. Without a pause, there would be no power to move forward—whether in fly-fishing or in life. This was one of those times that I gave myself permission to step back and allow the natural instinct to rest, trusting that when the time was right I'd move with fresh momentum into my life.

As I sat very still I allowed my mind to wander, and it led me to thoughts of work ethic and my resistance to take a break. I always saw myself as a high achiever, striving for high marks, winning awards and choosing an esteemed career in nursing. I did set an unusually high standard of excellence for myself and had been taught that if you were going to do a job you needed to do it right. I was proud of my successes, but in that moment something seemed off. It was the motivation behind these accomplishments that didn't feel authentic. It was as if I was chasing success and

I was one step behind. Not that I didn't experience it, but when I got there it didn't quite register or make me feel like I thought it would. I never felt like I was enough, and I was always trying to prove my worth. I was constantly searching for acceptance and appreciation from external sources. Maybe if I had focused on valuing and nurturing who I was and what I wanted, I would be in a different place.

I was tired. Not the kind of fatigue from lack of sleep, but the weariness that comes from always being on the go, staying busy, never feeling caught up. I felt depleted, like something was missing, and I decided I just didn't want to work hard. The minute I had that thought a second one popped in that I was being lazy and too much of a diva. I decided to explore my beliefs about work to get some clarity around my uneasiness.

Since I was born and raised on the farm, I learned that to do a good day's work you get up early, always stayed busy, had little down time, and at the end of a very long shift you fell in to bed and slept because when dawn came you got to do it all over again. I always remarked that my mom and dad got more done in the morning than I did all day. I don't remember a lot of time for relaxation or vacations—or fun. There were good times, but it seemed to me that they were over shadowed by struggle, responsibility, and hard work. I believed that it was virtuous to keep your nose to the grindstone. Work was meant to be arduous and getting lots done meant a sense of accomplishment. I knew the farm life was not for me when I was in my early teens. I was looking for way more excitement, travel, laughter, and fun than I witnessed. A sense of guilt crept in that I would feel this about a way of life that had been in my family for four generations. But pride swelled as I thought of my heritage, realizing while it might not be the way of life I chose, I was still glad it was part of who I was.

Part of my ultimate self-care was having the courage to choose a life and work that nourished my soul. I believe that my grandparents, parents, and brothers had chosen that by farming. I chose differently. By doing work that I was passionate about, I could have a lot more of that fun and laughter I was looking for. I was actually energized when I did things that I liked to do.

When I started my own business, I had the idea that in order to be successful I was going to have to put in eighty hours to avoid a forty-hour workweek as an employee. At first I struggled because I was really resistant to those kinds of hours and when I wasn't focusing on work, I felt guilty. If I wasn't sitting at my desk, presenting a seminar, or working on marketing and sales opportunities, I was thinking I should be doing more. It didn't help that when Stewart left the house in the morning, he would ask, "Are you working today?" His question irritated me because it touched on my own sensitivity that I wasn't moving forward fast enough to provide a second income to the family. A sense of urgency to get things accomplished, to always be working, and to reach goals left me feeling overwhelmed more frequently than not, which in turn kept me from taking action. I recognized the pattern of unworthiness and procrastination as my subconscious' way of keeping me in that space.

As an entrepreneur, I also had the idea that I had to do it all myself, even the stuff I wasn't good at or didn't like. *There's that streak of independence.* But the most profound realization was the belief system that taught me I had to pay my dues, life is tough, and nothing comes easy. I went into business with the thought that if it wasn't a struggle, I wasn't doing it right. At some point in my life, I learned that hard work was a virtue, and quite honestly, I didn't want it to be gruelling and unfulfilling. I acknowledged that there were some pretty negative thoughts and beliefs around work and struggle. Aversions and negativity led to misery. A change in perspective was definitely on the agenda.

Accomplishments, awards, and money had been measures I used to determine my success. I also recognized how attached I was to job titles as a sign of status. It was how I proved my worth. *It's no wonder I'm tired and struggling if I am constantly trying to prove something or have others see my value. If I don't recognize my own worth and constantly feel like I don't measure up then, it is not them I am trying to prove it to—it is me. It feels like there is no end in sight. It's not about the physical work, it is about the mental anguish, pressure, and emotions that I don't like. It's not the job; it's the meaning I give to it or the motivation behind it. If I could feel that I am enough—regardless of accomplishments, or jobs, or success then I wouldn't be craving approval, love, and acceptance. I wonder what it would be like if I stopped trying to prove myself and did work on my terms?*

This quiet time gave me the opportunity to determine my idea of success for my life and my business. *What do you want, Carla?* The corners of my mouth turned up as I thought of the familiar question from my forays into personal growth. *Why is this question always popping up?* I still struggled to find an answer. I had long ago stopped paying attention to my own dreams and desires and lived in default mode. It was easier to determine what I didn't want, and that was part of what led me to the depression. Staying stuck in negativity and focusing on choices that I made to get endorsements, to prove my value, or to fulfill someone else's image of who I am was my *modus operandi.*

While part of me was resistant to arduous work, I recognized that I liked challenges and felt a rush of adrenaline when working on a project I really connected with. There were glimpses of enjoyment when I put my attention on activities I was passionate about. When I was doing what I loved, work felt more like play. That went against what I had been taught. Yet, I was beginning to realize that I was working a good deal of my time and didn't even recognize it as such. I was actually doing more work than I was giving myself credit.

I thought of a plaque I had on my wall at home, *"It's not about finding yourself, it's about creating yourself."* I needed to ponder how I wanted to create myself daily rather than move through my life thinking my life was just going to happen on its own. I had the power to choose deliberately rather than continue to follow the old rules, roles, and expectations. Just as I shifted my position to ponder a response to my questions, the chanting began, signaling the end of our meditation session.

Before we were dismissed from the hall, we were called by name to sit at the front in groups of four. I took my place and waited calmly for the teacher to question my progress. I wondered if she would make any reference to the two incidents of vomiting I had experienced. Instead Sharon asked, "Carla, are you experiencing the sensations in your body?" I responded, "Yes." The interaction was to the point, but I felt like we had an inside secret. Only Sharon, Melanie, and Veronica were aware that I had been physically releasing my *saṅkhāras*. I kept my answer brief and subdued for the inquiry. These gatherings at the front of the room didn't seem like the time for a big discussion. Even though I had been interacting with Sharon and Melanie, I wanted to follow the decorum of silence in the hall. It seemed everyone followed and responded in one word or very brief sentences. My roommate, Veronica responded the same as the first few times. She described it as electricity moving through her. I could now relate to that response because I had experienced that feeling of flow, although not as electricity but more like warm syrup. I hadn't shared that description with the group, and surprisingly I didn't feel the need to.

Once all of the participants had their turn at the front, Sharon gave instructions to continue meditation in the hall or in the place of our choosing. Again, I didn't want to return to my room, so I wandered to the dining area. Outside the big window was another cold and stormy day. From the warmth inside, I watched as the snow fell gently and lightly next to the house, but at the end of the property and across the field, the wind was churning that white powder into a blustering dense wall and limited visibility. I was struck by the metaphor that inside the house was warm, safe, and peaceful. On the exterior of the building, but still close to the inner sanctuary, it was somewhat calm and clear even with the precipitation falling. The further away I looked there was less clarity, more confusion, and chaos.

I related my life to the storm. When I focused my attention on honouring my wants and needs I felt a sense of inner peace. Being clear about my thoughts and beliefs gave me courage to be authentic. I realized—it's all about me. No one else can make me happy and constantly looking for validation from others would only bring more misery. At the retreat, I had been working on happiness from the inside out, getting to peace, and harmony even with turmoil that might be outside of me. As I climbed the stairs to wash up before lunch I did feel lighter and more tranquil.

I took five minutes to lie down on my cot before the lunch gong rang. I didn't rush to get up and enjoyed the feeling of leisure that someone else was preparing my meal, and I just had to show up. I knew everyone would be lined up to go through the buffet procession, so I enjoyed the luxury of a pause. When I felt ready, I sauntered down the stairs to the dining area. After getting my food and settling on one of the stools, I looked discreetly around the room. I'm not sure what made me decide to observe my surroundings, but something made me raise my head and notice the others with me. Normally, I had been focusing my attention on my food, so I didn't inadvertently make eye contact. I was aware of the presence of others but had not really made a point of watching them. But what I did notice was Rochelle's absence. *Maybe she's in the washroom or not feeling well.* I wanted to ask out loud if anyone knew where she was, and I felt a twinge of worry. I found myself rushing through my food to investigate her absence. Trying to be inconspicuous I strolled past her bedroom on the main floor. Rochelle's cot was empty, and the luggage was gone.

A rush of disappointment flooded over me and I felt a strong urge to cry. I was sad that she had not made it through the full ten days and would not be there at the end to celebrate the accomplishment. We had talked about going for coffee and visiting after we finished the retreat. I regretted that we wouldn't have the chance to do that. And even more than that, her sudden departure triggered a feeling of abandonment. *How could I feel such an attachment to someone I had met only eight days earlier and spoken with for only a few hours?* There had been a strong and instantaneous connection, and her departure fractured the sense of kinship we had enjoyed. Remembering her gesture from the day before, I wondered if that was her way of saying goodbye.

Returning to my spot in front of the window I watched the storm and felt gloomy. A man was wandering out in the yard and his gait was erratic as he zigzagged and stumbled through the snow. He would stop for long periods of time and look up toward the sky. It almost looked like he was talking to himself or maybe to God, but he definitely appeared to be working off some excess energy. I turned from the window and climbed the stairs to my room. Several people were pacing around the common areas, and even I couldn't quite put my finger on why, but I sensed a collective agitation within the confines of our space. As I stretched out on my cot, I tried to regain the serenity I experienced earlier in the day. I was working hard to be equanimous about Rochelle's departure and the abandonment I felt.

I remember a quote once about people entering our lives for a reason, a season, or a lifetime. Reflecting on the day we arrived, when I struck up a conversation with Rochelle, I felt an immediate kinship. I acknowledged that I had been longing for some kind of support for what I deemed to be a challenge. I opened up to her and she to me—which was something I had guarded against for many years because it made me feel vulnerable. I thought this might be a friendship that started at the retreat and carried on into the future. When Rochelle left I felt a sense of loss because I had set up expectations for our relationship and those would not be fulfilled. The bell rang interrupting my thoughts of attachment. As I left my room and made my way to the meditation hall, I wondered how to connect without attachment.

The last sit of the day, I was back to embracing the technique, as Goenka stated in the opening of meditation, "Begin again, work diligently, observe the sensations." I focused intently on scanning and felt compelled to shut off the thoughts that had been occupying my mind. I became aware of the flow of energy and was comforted by a process that allowed me a distraction from my head by tuning into my body. For the second time that day, the pain in my side came on suddenly. I deepened my breathing, shifted my position in case I needed to bolt and waited. This time the pain dissipated without the need to vomit. I let out an audible sigh and nearly giggled out loud. The intensity of the pain decreased, and so did the drama associated with it. I saw this as a sign of progress.

The rest of the day was uneventful, and I longed for the discourse to start so I could tune into the teachings and focus on the wisdom. I had very much enjoyed the evening classes and listening to Goenka's stories to illustrate his points. When the bell rang, I was sitting on the couch in the dining area, having parked myself there after the afternoon meal. The usual procession started down the stairs and I fell into line.

"The eighth day is over. You have only two days left. You have only one day to work seriously. If one works seriously and exactly as the technique wants you to work, you get so much benefit and one day will be enough," Goenka started reassuringly. *I'm on the home stretch now. I hope the next few days go quickly. I'm ready to be done—ready to go home.* He continued on to say that there were two important techniques that we had been learning that would help us when we returned to our lives outside the retreat. First was awareness and second was equanimity.

Goenka likened them to the wings of a bird. Both needed to be equal in size and strength or the bird cannot fly. If we were aware of sensations, but generated cravings or aversions to them, then we were not practicing equanimity. Conversely, if we were calm and not reacting, but didn't pay attention to our vibrations then the purpose was not served.

He continued, "Awareness of the sensations on the body and equanimity of the sensations, pleasant or unpleasant, are the two wheels on the cart." We were cautioned that often what happens is we experience the unpleasant gross sensations like pain, and we tolerate them because we expect them to pass. When the subtle, more pleasant flow of energy comes, it is easy to become attached to it and want it to stay. Recognizing that all of these are not eternal and will come and go is part of the process. I smirked when Goenka said, "Deep rooted *saṅkhāras* will come to the surface in the form of gross sensations." *It was gross all right!* He continued to explain that the unconscious mind is constantly in touch with the body sensations and keeps on reacting as part of a habit pattern. If I recognize that it is not permanent and therefore no need to react I could come out of my misery.

Goenka added, "The law of nature is such that once you stop generating new sankharas, the old ones start coming up on the surface, get eradicated, and if you remain equanimous they continue to arise but get weaker, weaker, weaker, and get evaporated." *That is consistent with what I experienced. If I started seeing things as they are, not right or wrong and not good or bad, then that means I am not reacting. That would be completely liberating. I wonder if I will be able to take this learning and apply it to my life?* Goenka used the example of negativity being like a fire. If anger is the source of ignition or *saṅkhāra*, there is a biochemical reaction that happens within the body. If I make a choice to not react, then the blaze dies down because there is no fuel to sustain it. However, if I react and add some hurt feelings, maybe throw in a little resentment, I continue to put logs on the flames and soon I have a raging bonfire. Multiplication of the negativity will continue if I keep on reacting. *Definitely something I need to work on.*

The discourse ended with Goenka's usual blessing in his mother tongue, "May all beings be happy." I happily responded with the group, "Sadhu, sadhu, sadhu," meaning, "Well said, well done, we agree, and we share this wish."

As I climbed the stairs for some much-needed slumber, I basked in a newfound happiness.

Simple Steps to Reignite Your Soul Care

Stir Your Soul | Concentrate on creating the self, rather than finding the self.

Power Up Your Potential | Focus on valuing and nurturing who you truly are, rather than searching for acceptance and appreciation from external sources.

Activate Your Awareness | Become aware of your attachments and your aversions. What do you love and feel that you couldn't live without? Create a YES list. What do you despise and want no part of? Create a NO list.

Rock Your Resilience | Open your mind and consider how you have grown to appreciate something that you once didn't like at all. How did that shift occur?

Kick Ass With Intentional Action | Look in the mirror and again observe without judgement. The ultimate in self-care is caring for the soul, the spirit, rather than caring for the exterior alone as many of us do. Say something kind to your reflection and accept the compliment graciously.

Day Nine

"If your mind carries a heavy burden of the past, you will experience more of the same. The past perpetuates itself through lack of presence. The quality of your consciousness at this moment is what shapes the future."

Eckhart Tolle, The Power of Now: A Guide to Spiritual Enlightenment

"Imagine my surprise when I found joy had been inside me all along. I just had to reconnect with it."

Day 9

Reignite Your Happiness

I was dreaming when the bell woke me at four. I don't remember the dream, but it was pleasant because I drifted into consciousness with a calm and peaceful feeling. As I opened my eyes and looked around the room, it took a few minutes to orient myself and remember that my time at the retreat was nearly over. Resolving to stay up and meditate rather than crawl back in bed, I headed to the bathroom. A long hot shower to wash away the last of my sleepiness was the key to following through with my intentions. As the water cascaded over my skin, I focused on the sensations of warmth and flow. There was something relaxing about being aware of what I was feeling. It was a rare moment of presence. I couldn't help but think of the first days at the retreat when I had eagerly prepared for the day and my mind had been racing. There had been a sense of urgency to get to the meditation hall and get to work. Now I was blanketed in serenity.

It was 4:50 a.m. by the time I was done in the bathroom, and I was completely alert. Veronica had already gone to the hall, and I decided to take advantage of the empty room. I turned on the lights to stay awake and climbed on my bed. Propping my pillow against the wall as a backrest, I assumed my meditation position. To settle my mind, I did a few minutes of Anapana meditation that we had learned in the first days, focusing on the upper lip area below my nose to notice the sensations of my breath moving in and out. Within a few minutes, I moved into the Vipassana technique of scanning my body for sensations. I felt the familiar flow in areas like my chest, arms, and legs. I had an occasional itch or twinge, but no pain, and I was able to observe and not react. The ringing of the breakfast bell startled me, bringing me out of my blissful awareness. I had been completely absorbed in the meditation.

Leaving my room, I paused for a moment in the hallway that overlooked the dining area. I counted the number of women to see if anyone else had departed. A fleeting thought of Rochelle crossed my mind, and I hoped that she was doing OK. I carried on down the stairs for the morning sustenance. My mind drifted as I crunched on the granola and almond milk, and I imagined how good my first cup of Tim Hortons' brewed coffee would taste in forty-eight hours. I hadn't minded the various flavours of herbal tea and instant decaf coffee, but I missed the strong aroma and first sips of liquid caffeine. It was a morning ritual that I looked forward to resuming.

The food had been a pleasant surprise at the retreat. As a farm girl raised on plenty of meat, the idea of rapidly converting to a vegetarian diet had been a concern prior to embarking on the journey. Aside from the pasty morning oatmeal, there was only one day where I had abstained from what was prepared. I couldn't get past the texture of tofu, and it was offered as an addition to the miso soup that had accompanied the salad. Fortunately, the pan of white gelatinous goo was on the side, and I was able to just sip on the broth. That was the only day that I truly missed having a nice chicken breast or meat in general.

Breakfast had been served at 6:30 a.m. and lunch at 11:00 a.m. They were our largest meals. Tea break was from 5:00 to 6:00 p.m. daily. Instead of the large dinner that I would have had at home, we were served only tea and fresh fruit. The returning students were only provided tea or lemon water. There was no snacking in between meals. At the beginning of the retreat, I was worried that I would feel famished with this drastic change to my eating habits.

Yet during the entire time I was there, I do not remember at any time feeling hungry. It had been a positive experience overall, but I had no plans of continuing with the vegetarian lifestyle once I left the retreat behind. I was happy to comply with the tradition to not eat meat since it violated one of the precepts to not kill any being; however, I had been learning to make choices based on my own needs and wants—not on the rules and beliefs of others. Embracing the idea that this was the right decision for me, I felt my mouth water as I thought of my first meal post retreat—a serving of beef with creamy mashed potatoes and vegetables.

After breakfast, I lingered over a second cup of instant coffee while I sat in front of the large window watching the sky brighten. The storm from the day before had passed, and the weather appeared to be nice enough for a walk outside. I was wrong. All bundled up, I stepped out anticipating it to be cold, but not expecting the deep freeze that smacked me in the face. Inside the compound, where several of the cars were parked, the snow had completely drifted over top of one of the vehicles. An attempt had been made to shovel it off, but to no avail. I giggled out loud. *If people wanted to leave, the universe certainly wasn't making it easy for them.* Glancing at my van parked on the street, I wondered if it would start due to the extreme temperatures. It was a fleeting thought. I had no intentions of leaving—particularly now. With the cold air burning inside my chest as it entered my lungs and ice crystals forming on my face, I had no other choice than to quickly escape the frigid outdoors and take refuge in the warmth of the house. I was refreshed and ready to head into the meditation hall for the morning sit.

Still shivering a little, I sat in the dining area waiting for the gong to ring—the traditional signal for participants to make their way to the basement. I was eager to get to my spot, wrap myself in the flannel blanket, and ease into the next hour of meditation. After experiencing the glacial air outside the house, the cooler temperature of the hall seemed warm. As the chanting started, a thought popped into my head: *Everything depends on my perspective. I remember thinking that it was cold in the basement when I came from the warmth of the main house, but now when I had ventured to a colder place before entering the sanctuary, the temperature felt like it was different. If I looked at events in my life and the stories I created around them, I could choose to view them from a fresh approach. By seeing things in a different light, this new illumination showed me that I had the power and the responsibility to change my perspective if I wanted to be happy. No one else could make that happen for me.*

I was in analytical mode and took a deep breath to refocus and work on scanning for sensations. I enjoyed the feeling of subtle vibrations throughout my body but was careful to not get too attached to them as Goenka had cautioned the night before. I soon heard the familiar chanting to signal the end of meditation. *That was fast!* Sharon then spoke, telling us we could meditate in the place of our choosing.

I decided to return to my room and stretch out on the bed. I had full intentions to continue with contemplation but found myself drifting off to sleep. I didn't fight the urge. I crawled under the covers, assumed a fetal position, and took a delightful nap. I slept soundly and was awakened by the lunch bell an hour later.

As I ate my lunch and looked outdoors, I had a sudden ache in my chest and a flow of warmth start at the top of my head and move down my body. At exactly the same moment, I thought of my kids. *Holy crap! I miss them!* I fought the urge to cry.

I had never experienced such a wave of love and longing to be with them. I had a picture of them that was so vivid in my mind. I thought of Sianna—her big blue eyes and her long ginger hair that she had once grown out to donate to make wigs for cancer survivors. I reveled in the memory of bringing the twins home from the hospital. Rylee, twin A, because he was born first, was now tall and athletic with dark hair and brown eyes like Stew. Shaelyn, twin B, resembled Sianna with the hair and eye color, but had a completely different personality. I smiled when I thought of how she was always on the go for one social occasion or another. I was beaming with pride as I rejoiced silently about my amazing children.

As I continued to sit in the dining area after lunch, I considered the wave of strong emotion I had about my kids. I had been travelling extensively in the year prior to the retreat.

There were times that I thought about them and even missed seeing them, but I had not experienced that sense of yearning to be with them, to hold them, and to tell them I loved them—no matter how long I had been gone. I wondered if I was having withdrawal symptoms from no talking and no physical contact. *I sure want a hug.* Yet, the sentiment of the moment was deeper than a longing for a hug. I felt as though purging the pains and wounds that I had been carrying for so long opened up a space in my heart. But instead of a void because something was gone, it was filled with love and happiness. It was as though the clouds had parted long enough for sunshine to pour in. Then a rush of love, that was there all along, illuminated that space.

Reflecting on my time as a mother, it had started with heartache and disappointment when the first two babies I carried did not survive. When I became pregnant with Sianna, I shared my fears and anxiety with no one, including my husband. I did not allow myself the joy of pregnancy or the wonder of what my newborn would be like. I would not let myself become attached or fall in love for worry that once again I would experience loss. Even after the tests confirmed that she was a healthy baby, I couldn't bring myself to let my guard down. So I ate to numb the emotions. I gained sixty pounds and ignored Doctor Wong when he chastised me saying, "Too much cookies and ice cream!"

I retorted, "I don't eat cookies or ice cream."

He shook his head in disgust because we both knew I was eating everything else I could get my hands on.

I felt as though I was on edge, almost holding my breath continually through the pregnancy. As the days led up to my due date, I put a smile on my face and acted excited, but inside the anxiety built. I was induced for three days—yes, three days—and after a difficult labor, I delivered our beautiful nine-pound, three-ounce baby. Instead of noticing joy and love as I held her and marveled at her beauty, I let go a sigh of relief. For the first time in nine months, I could breathe again. Sianna was an amazing baby, and I enjoyed the first year of motherhood to the point where I decided to be weaned off the antidepressants I had been taking for over a year.

My diagnosis was two years before, but I refused the medication because I felt the anxiety and depression were strictly situational—intense stress and unresolved conflict at work had me completely overwhelmed. I went from that experience to our personal crisis with the babies. It was only when I was emotionally preparing to get pregnant for a third time that I agreed to go on the pills.

I read an article, describing women who struggled with infertility becoming pregnant after being treated for depression. At this point, I was willing to try anything to get pregnant again.

The first two times I had conceived very quickly, but the third time was taking a while, and I was frustrated. I went to see my doctor and asked, "Do you think I'm still depressed?" Doctor O'Connor graciously smiled. "You've been through a lot and I think the medication could help." Along with the pharmaceutical treatment, he referred me for therapy. All of which I started diligently and within a few weeks, I was pregnant for the third time. When it had all turned out so well and I had my beautiful little girl, I thought I was "fixed" so the weaning from the meds seemed like the next logical step.

It didn't take long for the feeling of discontent and sadness to come back. I was angry with myself for being so ungrateful. I tried to understand how I had everything I thought I wanted yet could not experience the happiness I longed for. My fabulous life was shrouded in a cloak of dissatisfaction. Something was missing. I talked about going back to work and did do some corporate health consulting for a short period of time. My previous boss at the Occupational Health Centre had also called several times to talk about opportunities, but I wasn't sure that was what I wanted, mainly because I didn't take the time to figure out what I did want. Little did I realize that I didn't have the luxury of figuring that out because life was about to get a whole lot more hectic.

I suspected I was pregnant when we were in Toronto attending a conference for Stew's work. I had to fight back tears and swallow a big lump in my throat during the national anthem to keep from becoming a sobbing mess during the opening ceremonies. The second clue came when we attended the formal gala. As we stood in the crowd watching a Cher impersonator, I turned to Stew and said, "Hold my drink. I'm going to faint." The next thing I knew my arms were draped over the shoulders of Stew and Hal, and they were dragging me through the crowd. Once clear of the stifling throngs of people, I caught my breath and felt fine. Stew said it was because of the body shaper and form fitting dress I wore that I couldn't breathe. Our friend Hank diagnosed me and said, "You're knocked up for sure." I confirmed my pregnancy as soon as we got home, and I soon added another reason to be concerned when at seven weeks I found out I was carrying twins.

The fear and anxiety were back with vengeance since I had not one but two little souls to worry about. Each appointment and medical test was approached with cautious optimism, but an underlying and insidious sense of "what if it happens again?" loomed over me. Even when diagnostic reports indicated that the babies were healthy, and I was in good physical condition, worry plagued my thoughts. I asked to go back on the antidepressants. In the two weeks before delivery, I was hospitalized to have continuous testing on the babies' status. It was easy to remain very detached and clinical while the staff would attach two Doppler's to my abdomen and watch the monitor to ensure that the babies were not in distress. They monitored me too— physically. Emotionally, I pretended that I was fine because I was making a conscious effort to not focus on what I was really feeling. My daily medication helped me to ignore the fear and uncertainty that had become dominant in my gynecological experience.

Then I got tired of waiting for these little ones to arrive, so during one of my day passes from the hospital, I decided to help nature along. I had received some advice from the midwife at the hospital regarding several things I could try to bring on labour. She suggested a long walk, having intercourse, and the good old standby, a healthy dose of Castor oil. Since my feet were the size of cantaloupes and I waddled with the girth of a heifer, the first two options were not appealing. So I downed a shot glass of the thick, clear, putrid emollient, and chased it with a tall glass of pink grapefruit juice. I returned to the hospital for the night and waited for the action to start.

By the early morning hours, I called Stew, who was at home, and asked him to come in. He got there in time to hold my hand while the anesthesiologist inserted the needle in my back for the epidural. I was sitting up in bed, calmly visiting with Stew and feeling no pain when Dr. Wong came in and did an internal exam. His comment, "She's ten," started a flurry of activity that I watched as though I was an uninvolved onlooker. Stew and I occasionally glanced at each other and smiled as the room filled with people and equipment. Dr. Wong had a nurse to assist him, and there was another to do the recording in the chart, the pediatrician, a respiratory therapist, and one nurse for each baby after delivery. One of my favourite nurses, Marge—an experienced midwife—

stayed on shift to be my personal nurse and labour coach. Stew needed little direction from Marge and coached me like a pro, holding my hand, giving me ice chips, sharing witty insights and comments to encourage the excitement of the event. Stew tried to engage Dr. Wong in some light banter, but the physician was all business. If Stew had any apprehension, it did not show, and since it was not our practice to share deep emotions, it never occurred to me to ask how he was doing.

When the first baby was born everyone marveled at his size and took guesses at the weight before the nurse announced he weighed eight pounds two ounces. Dr. Wong shook his head, "Too much cookies and ice cream." I didn't care. They took twin A out of the room to check him and also make space for the second warmer to be rolled in for twin B's arrival. She was in no hurry, and thirteen minutes later my smallest baby at six pounds ten ounces was delivered safe and sound. Now I could breathe that big sigh of relief I had waited so long for.

Looking out at the yard blanketed with the frosty snow, I reflected that the surge of love and strong emotion I felt earlier in the day was something that I had not allowed myself to experience even as my healthy, beautiful children grew and developed. I could blame it on being too busy with diapers and bottles, while looking after the house, but that wouldn't be the truth. I didn't doubt that I loved my kids, but I didn't know how to connect deeply with them. Allowing myself to feel this kind of love meant that I would be vulnerable, and my heart would be exposed to potential pain. I had glimpses of grief but had never fully immersed myself in it. I hadn't allowed it to pass through me to complete the process. For that matter, I had pushed away any intense emotions as soon as I felt them start to overwhelm me. I worried that I would be overcome and lose that precious sense of control that kept me in my comfort zone. So I avoided the feelings by keeping them at arm's length. Each time they bubbled up, I pushed them down.

I acknowledged that if I allowed myself to feel the sadness, shame, and guilt, the fear went away. The biggest fear—fear of expressing who I am at my core was also starting to dissipate.

I recognized that since I hadn't fully loved and accepted myself, I wasn't able to pass that on in a pure way to my husband or even my children. An even more startling realization had been that I had not let anyone love me. I remember being an assistant at one of Jack Canfield's events and having pressure build in my head. I had come to recognize the headache as a symptom that I was holding back emotion.

Previously my answer would have been to pop a few Tylenol and carry on. On that day, I approached my mentor Kathy and said, "I've got something brewing. I could use a RIM session." She was a master facilitator in The RIM Method—a guided imagery technique that helped process emotional obstacles. As I asked for help, I felt a small relief of the pounding in my head. When we found a quiet, private space and I allowed the thoughts, feelings, and tears to flow, a pressure valve loosened, and the intense sensation dissipated. The process clarified the root cause was of not knowing how to let people in—to let others love me.

I had robbed myself of experiencing the joys of my children's childhood, and in doing so I had denied myself happiness and love. No wonder I was depressed. I tried to fix myself with antidepressants, but that was just putting a Band-Aid on the issue—until that day five years prior when I watched my children play in the backyard and realized that life is too precious to feel numb and empty. In that instance, I had a sense that I wanted more—for me and for my children. I hadn't known where to start or how I would find the happiness I longed for, but I knew then that I wanted a change. It had been a long and interesting journey from that initial moment of clarity to sitting at a silent meditation retreat. Imagine my surprise when I found joy had been inside me all along. I just had to reconnect with it.

Activity in the dining area brought me out of my thoughts, and I sensed the gong had sounded for the afternoon meditation. I took a few minutes before moving toward the hall.

Just as I had felt a shift in my energy after experiencing the vomiting episodes, the strong wave of love and subsequent understanding of its meaning made an impact, and I wanted to bask in it for a moment longer. I was the last person to descend for our final group sit of the day. A sense of contentment surrounded me as I settled on my cushion and waited for Goenka's chanting to initiate the session. I settled in and became aware of the sensations in my body for the next hour.

When the chanting cued the completion of our sit, I felt like I was just getting in to the flow.

I remained in the hall once Sharon released us from the group meditation. I sat on my cushion and focused my attention on my breathing. It was slow and deep, and as I drifted into a state of complete relaxation, the word "presence" floated through my mind. I think that was the essence of the teachings I had been learning during my time of silence. By shutting out the chaos of the external world and clearing the wounds of the past, I learned to be in the moment—to allow myself to feel the emotions and sensations in my body because they would give me the answers to how I wanted to show up in my life. And how I wanted to show up was to have more love and more laughter. The laughter would have to wait until I was no longer under the constraints of Noble Silence. The love I could experience right away.

I returned to my room to freshen up before afternoon tea. I was counting the hours now until we would be allowed to talk and interact. I had enough of the quiet contemplation and felt as though I had made some really good progress since my first days at the retreat. As I wandered downstairs for the discourse, I looked forward to the jovial teachings Goenka would share with us to close the ninth day.

He started our evening session by encouraging us to understand how we could use Vipassana in our day-to-day life. As he said, "It is an art of living, how to live a proper life, a harmonious life, a peaceful life." As I listened to Goenka speak, I thought of how I did feel different, but I questioned if I would be able to maintain this sense of serenity, peace, and happiness when I was once again exposed to the busyness of the outside world.

Goenka explained that we tend to turn to something pleasurable like going out dancing, to the movies, or to the bar to divert our attention from our misery. I was thinking things like using alcohol or other drugs to numb the pain or anger and distance us from our unhappiness. For years I used, medication, food and long hours of mindless TV as my distractions. Stuffing and ignoring had been my ways to deal or not-deal with the toxic thoughts and beliefs that kept me stuck in a cycle of negativity and self-loathing.

I had pushed anger, guilt, shame, resentment and fear from my conscious mind deep into my subconscious mind where it could fester and build. The result was depression, fragile relationships, and a bad habit of not taking care of myself. By disconnecting it was a form of escaping and hiding and I had figured out that wasn't the solution to my problem. I don't want to live my life like that anymore. If I want happiness and joy, then I need to make the choice to heal and come out from hiding.

The guru instructed, "Whenever any negativity arises, don't suppress and don't give it the free license to express at the vocal level or the physical level." He cautioned that we could still expect to have anger, worry, guilt, and fear come up in life, but the difference is in our response to what we were feeling. We could do what we had been taught, to simply observe. I saw this as a type of learning opportunity, to use the emotions I was feeling to draw my attention to something I needed to be aware of. Through my experience at the retreat, I noticed that sensations become weaker and went away when I just allowed them. I didn't need to fear them so much as I needed to learn from them.

"Vipassana helps you to see what is happening inside which is more important than what is happening outside," the teacher explained. *It's all a story I tell myself, how I interpret what is happening in my surroundings. If I focus on my response, I am completely able to make a change if needed.*

Goenka described that when we came to the retreat we thought that one hundred percent of our misery was caused by outside situations, people, and experiences. One of the most profound statements of the whole retreat rang in my ears when he said, "Nothing outside can make you miserable just like nothing outside can make you happy. The cause of happiness and misery lies inside."

It seems so simple. The stories and drama I have created can all be changed. I don't think I would call it easy, but it is certainly doable. I had searched the depths of my mind, excised old and unresolved pains, and was coming out the other side with a different perspective. The chanting concluded the discourse as Goenka sang his closing, *Bhaavatu sabba mańgalam*—May all beings be happy!

As I ascended the stairs to my room, I thought how the kids count the number of sleeps until Christmas. *One more sleep till I get to talk; two more sleeps till I get to go home.* I basked in a sense of contentment and pride that I had made it to the end of the Noble Silence. As I prepared for bed and climbed in for slumber, I noticed that my mind was clear and settled.

I took a few deep breaths and felt my body relax further into the cot. I pulled the covers up under my chin and drifted easily off to sleep.

Simple Steps to Reignite Your Happiness

Stir Your Soul | Only by fully loving and accepting yourself can you fully love and accept others.

Power Up Your Potential | Acknowledge that you are *deserving* of happiness and of everything you've ever wanted from life.

Activate Your Awareness | Joy has been inside of you all along; you simply need to reconnect with it.

Rock Your Resilience | Emptying your mind and heart of old pains and wounds allows that space to be filled with love and happiness.

Kick Ass With Intentional Action | Do one thing this week, simply because it brings you joy.

Day Ten

"I've begun to realize that you can listen to silence and learn from it. It has a quality and a dimension all its own"

Chaim Potok, The Chosen

"In the silence I had heard the voice of my soul, so I didn't have the strong need to hear it out loud. The once feared quiet was now welcomed because I was, perhaps for the first time in my life, comfortable with being me!"

Day 10

Reignite Your Relationships

I opened my eyes slowly and smiled. This was the day that I was going to talk and interact with the other participants. As I laid in the dark waiting for the morning gong to ring, I took a deep breath and appreciated the silence. I knew that in a few hours the peace and serenity would be inundated with chatter. Part of me was excited to hear my fellow participants share their experiences, and the other was a little sad that quiet camp was drawing to a close. Stepping out of my busy life and into the serenity and calmness of this haven had reenergized me and given me an opportunity to reflect and connect with a deeper part of who I was. Prior to falling asleep, I had a fleeting concern about whether I would be able to sustain the benefits I felt from the retreat experience. This doubt lingered as a backdrop to the excitement.

I turned on my side and watched as Veronica climbed out of bed after the bell rang. I pulled the covers up and considered whether to go to the meditation hall or snuggle deeper into the warmth. I felt alert and knew that the hours to share meditation energy with the others were limited so I got dressed and headed downstairs once Veronica finished in the bathroom. As I entered the dim basement, I saw there wouldn't be as much energy as I thought. Only a few other people showed up. It was simply an observation. I was unconcerned about the attendance as I positioned myself on the cushion of comfort and delved into the sensations. An hour later, I felt complete.

As I wandered by the bulletin board, I noticed that for the first time in nine days the schedule was different. The daily activities were only provided up to nine a.m. and then the itinerary was blank. *Hallelujah!* I squealed an internal scream of relief. I anticipated that this would be when we were released from our vow of Noble silence. With a skip in my step, I returned to my room until breakfast.

After showering, I descended the grand stairway to the dining area, pausing to sense if the energy in the room felt different, if there might be excitement from someone other than me. I believed that the buzz of anticipation I felt existed in the others as well, but I didn't feel any difference as I moved through the buffet line to get my morning meal. The proof of eagerness came after breakfast when a majority of the women milled about in the dining hall rather than retreating to their respective bedrooms as they had done on previous days. It seemed I wasn't the only one ready to get to the talking!

As we had done so many times in the past days, we descended single file to one of our last meditations as a group. I settled on my cushion, felt the firm support of the wall behind me, and smiled at the memory of asking to be moved to this spot earlier in my stay. How different my experience in the meditation hall was now compared to the very first day. I was limber and could sit for an hour without moving to get comfortable, and I had purged toxic thoughts and beliefs—literally and figuratively. There were some significant memories and emotions that I was able to process, healing many of my past wounds. My racing mind had been reinvented as a calmer, more patient tool, and I felt refreshed and reenergized. I fairly consistently had awareness of sensations through my body, and when I didn't that was okay, too. I smiled, mentally patting myself on the back for making it ten days with limited interaction and very little talking. I acknowledged that I was okay with not being perfectly quiet the entire time because I remained within the rules of the retreat. I continued reminiscing about the experience of the last few days rather than focusing on meditation, and I was totally at peace with that. Then I felt a flutter of eagerness as Goenka's voice chimed in to signal the end of the group meditation hour.

Sharon advised all of us that we were to maintain the sanctity of silence until we were at the top of the stairs and had entered the house. There was a sign propped on the floor as I walked through the garage stating, "Once inside the dining area you are now permitted to speak; however, please continue with the precept of no physical touch between participants." A question of "why" passed through my mind, but I carried on. I honestly had expected to burst through the door from the mudroom and pounce on the closest bystander. I envisioned a cartoon character staggering through a saloon-style swinging door, her head progressively enlarging like a balloon frantically searching for someone to grab and allow the words to come out of her mouth, letting the pressure off so her head would return to a normal size.

Instead, I slowly moved through the room looking at the displays of books and pictures that had been set up while we were in the basement. I noticed staff, absent during the retreat, now milled around the room. One of my fellow participants stood beside me, as I was absorbed in reading a poster. I was aware that when I started speaking that I was whispering. Even though I had contact with Sharon and Melanie at several times during the week, this was new. I felt almost shy. Having not met her at the beginning of our time I said, "I'm Carla. It's nice to finally meet you."

Jamie smiled as she introduced herself then leaned toward me, as if to tell me a secret and lowered her voice to ask, "How was your experience?"

A burst of laughter erupted. "Interesting, how was yours?" Suddenly, any hesitance to talk was gone as we dove into a detailed conversation.

She shared, "I'm a yoga teacher, and I have done meditation before so I thought this was going to be easy, but it was hard. I knew people who did this and talked about leaving or wanting to leave, and I was confident that wouldn't be me, but I did want to go numerous times."

I smiled as I observed Jamie, her long, dark hair pulled back in a high pony tail, clear luminous skin, and a petite, lean body dressed in Lulu active wear. She matched my vision of a yoga teacher. As I looked down at my own generic sweats and comfortable baggy sweat-shirt, I did not look like a yoga instructor, nor did I come into this thinking it was going to be easy, but I did feel a connection with my fellow participant about leaving.

"It was a challenge to stay. I thought about bolting a few times, but I knew I would be disappointed with myself if I didn't see it to the end. Besides, I wasn't too interested in rushing back to cooking, cleaning, and laundry!" I admitted.

She laughed and added, "Lots of old memories came up for me around past relationships that I sorted through and resolved."

"Yeah, I sorted through lots of old baggage and did some purging." I didn't expand, and it didn't seem to need explanation as my new friend nodded her head in understanding.

As Jamie and I talked, we migrated to the cream couch that had been a comforting place to sit during our times in the common area. Soon other women joined us, and we chatted, comparing stories and laughing. I loved the sense of camaraderie we shared and was surprised at the bond I felt with a group that I had spent more time with in silence than in conversation. The discussion was non-stop about comfort, discomfort, surprises, and awareness that each of us had. Nearly everyone in the circle shared a desire to escape at one time or another through the long days of contemplation.

Wow! So many stories with different details, yet there were similarities in the responses we had and the profound effect that the retreat had on each of us. It's not just me that is looking for the answers to living a happier and more fulfilling life.

I was particularly drawn to listen to Sandy's stories. She was in my small group when Sharon checked on our progress during sessions, and I commented, "Sandy, I was so impressed with your honesty about what was happening for you, when you shared your struggles and obstacles."

"That was nothing," she chortled. "Compared to what was happening in response to the food situation. For the first five days I couldn't go to the bathroom, and the minute we got in the hall the rumbling and growling on my insides was so loud I was sure everyone could hear. The poor girls in my room, I wanted to apologize for the gas, but couldn't say anything!"

By this point, I was in fits of laughter as she finished her explanation.

With a straight face and a momentary pause, Sandy carried on, "On day six, I discovered the Smooth Move tea, but it really should be called ex-lax in a cup! Then I had a different problem, and there was nothing smooth or gentle about it." Gales of giggles continued as she kept spouting hilarious one-liners regarding her digestive difficulties. I knew I had found a kindred spirit when she lamented, "I'm an Alberta girl. I can't wait to have a juicy, hamburger when I get out of here!" By the time the bell rang, and we were called for lunch, I had tears running down my face and a pain in my side—this time from pure joy and amusement.

The festive ambiance continued around the large dining table, and it reminded me of Christmas celebrations when our extended family of cousins, aunts, and uncles would share in the excitement of the holidays. Admittedly, having all of the participants together for the meal brought a different energy. Even though both sexes were present in the meditation hall for the past ten days, this was the first that we had actually interacted together as an entire group. Except for some of the women who had male partners there, the remaining females still congregated together and didn't integrate with our male counterparts. And once again, I acknowledged a sense of an unspoken bond. I listened, enjoying the revelry, and observed that as much as I had longed to be talking, in that moment I was content to not say anything. I was savouring a quiet peacefulness within, while observing the noise outside. This awareness made me think of my friend and mentor, Gary John, who described a similar experience after his thirty-day silent meditation experience. He told me, "I just didn't feel like I had anything that needed to be said." It wasn't until I had a similar experience that I understood what he was telling me.

After we cleared and washed our dishes, there was no need to retreat to our bedrooms in silence so we lingered over tea around the table like an ordinary kitchen party. At one point discussions were put on hold so that the representative from the Vipassana Association could talk briefly about how the retreats are funded through donations from people who have completed the ten days. There was no pressure, and we were asked to donate only what we felt we could easily afford and felt compelled to give. After the short presentation, participants returned to their discussions and wandered to make payment in their own time. I was happy to write a cheque to pay for someone else to attend, just as someone had done for me.

I excused myself to use the bathroom and when I returned to the dining area, I stood on the outskirts of the crowd, watching and listening. This was something new for me to step back, be quiet, and take in my surroundings. My tendency was to be right in the middle of the crowd talking, clowning around, and telling stories. That had been my way to connect with people. I was suddenly aware that it had also been my way to keep people at arms length. That chatter and revelry kept away the deep connection that could happen when I delved into the real feelings and vulnerability present in loving relationships.

Prior to coming to the retreat, quiet stillness freaked me out!

A fond memory of childhood popped in as I remembered sitting around the dinner table, all of us talking at once. It was loud and boisterous, just as we were in our everyday lives. I wanted to be seen and heard so I talked incessantly, which I recognized now as a plea for love and acknowledgment. We were all talking, but it was more like banter than deep meaningful conversations about what was really going on for each of us. The first time I actually spoke the words, "I love you," to my siblings was during toasts at their weddings, and each time I felt an overwhelming rush of emotion that choked me up so I could barely get the words out. Those cherished words were reserved for special occasions much like Mom's fine china. When I left home I lived in university residence, constantly surrounded by activity, noise, and people. I thrived, or so I thought.

Moving into an apartment by myself had been a challenge. I remember keeping the television on constantly to keep me company. Being around people and talking energized me. Yet, when I was in the depths of my depression, I had isolated myself from many friends and family. My pattern of disconnecting from people had never been clearer to me as when I spent a week in the presence of hundreds of people at Jack Canfield's Breakthrough to Success training—and I kept completely to myself. I would return to my room during breaks, eat by myself, and made few efforts to get to know anyone. This was a different type of being quiet—hiding and not being my gregarious self.

It was early in my personal transformation journey, and I had only been off the antidepressants for about a year so I was in transition from a numb, wounded shell of myself trying to claw my way back to the confident, fun-loving, energetic girl that I knew had existed in what seemed like a life time ago. I told myself that I was "playing full out," as Jack encouraged us to do. I did all of my homework, including the evening mirror talks, and participated in all the experiential exercises. I remember him saying on the first day, "Don't be the person who shows up and doesn't really do the work, only to have your breakthrough after you leave when you may not have support."

Well, I had my breakthrough or rather breakdown, at the very last minute. With less than forty-five minutes left of the seven-day workshop, we did a milling exercise that shattered my already fractured shield. We were to role-play with another participant, with them speaking encouraging words that we most wanted to hear from an important person in our life. I chose Stewart and asked her to express, "I love and appreciate you more than I ever let on." Short and to the point, then she requested that I act as her three grown children and had a long and detailed script that she wanted me to say. The tears started slowly as I spoke, then came the pauses to try and regain my composure. I was acutely aware of a throbbing headache and a lump in my throat that made it hard to swallow. By the time I finished telling her what she most wanted to hear, the two of us were hugging each other, sobbing openly and freely. I was having my breakdown.

After the exercise was over, I escaped to the bathroom, thinking that a moment to take a deep breath in privacy would help me put the shield firmly back in place. As I was heading back toward the conference room, one of the assistants asked if I was okay. I smiled politely and said, "Oh yes, I am totally fiiiinnne," as my composure once again crumbled and the end of the sentence was more of a guttural sound than a word.

Theresa put her arm around my shoulders and ushered me to a nearby couch. I felt no judgment from her as she sat quietly holding my hand and allowed me to release the sobs wracking my body. I felt safe and uninhibited to just let them come out. As my respirations slowed and the tears subsided, she asked, "Would you like to do a visualization?"

I started crying again and gasped between big gulps of air, "You don't understand. I have been doing meditation and visualizations all week." I took a big deep breath and continued with a bit more control, "I don't see a damn thing. I'm just not getting it. I don't think it will help."

She smiled reassuringly and in a smooth comforting maternal voice she said, "That's okay. How about I just talk you through some guided relaxation breathing?"

"Okay," I nodded, and we shared a few minutes of guided meditation. Thinking that the breakthrough was complete, I returned to the final minutes of the seminar and left promptly to my room to get ready for the banquet and Come as You'll be Party. It was short lived; I attended the party, quickly ate my dinner, and rushed back to my room, where I ran a hot bath and climbed in to finish the crying I started earlier. I sobbed for a long time, as grief oozed out of me. I didn't realize it at the time but reflecting on it now I had released some of the anger, regret, and sadness about the woman I had become that was so drastically different than the woman I wanted to be. It was a powerful transformational moment that inspired me to keep showing up for the journey of self-discovery.

After completing the Vipassana retreat, I had a new relationship with silence, one that provided me with security and comfort. While I had previously withdrawn from people and activities that brought me joy and happiness, the real issue was that *I had progressively lost connection to who I was and what I wanted.* I had let debilitating patterns and beliefs take hold to keep me in a pretty unhappy space. In the silence I had heard the voice of my soul, so I didn't have the strong need to hear it out loud. The urgency to be the centre of attention, through loud and boisterous conversations felt less important. The once feared quiet was now welcomed because I was, perhaps for the first time in my life, comfortable with being me!

As I stood in the doorway, Melanie walked up beside me and asked, "Are you okay?"

How many times has she had to check on me in the past few days? "I'm great. I was just enjoying the noise," I replied.

She continued, "I'm so glad you held out and stayed. Most people would have run!"

I laughed, "I did think about it a few times, but I didn't really ever entertain the idea seriously. Determination set in, and I really was excited that I had a physical and profound response. It helped me believe in the process, and better yet it's going to make a helluva story to tell!"

As we talked, Veronica joined in and concurred with Melanie's sentiment that she was happy I stayed and had been worried I would leave. "I knew you were going through something and throwing up, but you didn't seem sick. And your friend, she left on day eight."

I turned to Melanie and questioned her about Rochelle, "Was she okay when she left?"

Her description of the scene made me smile as she explained that Rochelle had requested to leave, and Melanie told us, "I did everything I could to convince her to stay." "I helped her carry her belongings to the vehicle and even joked with her that if her car didn't start, that was a sign she should stay." But it started, and she left. Melanie added, "She wanted me to pass on her phone number and to ask you to call her."

Melanie went to her room and returned quickly with a slip of paper the size of a fortune cookie insert. I tucked it in my pocket and later put it in my room. I had full intentions of following up with my friend, but by the time I arrived home I had misplaced the number and had no way of contacting Rochelle—I didn't even know her last name.

The gong rang, and Sharon announced that we would be having an afternoon group meditation. It felt strange to go from the boisterous noise of the common area and submerge into silence as we each crossed the threshold to the hall. The shift in energy felt like the first time we had entered the hall together ten days earlier, and for a fleeting moment, it made me feel like we were going backwards rather than preparing to go home. On the first evening when we had done the exact same thing, I was filled with anticipation, excitement, and a little anxiety about what I was getting myself into. As I descended into the sanctuary, I felt calm, centered and a sense of security, much like I anticipated returning home would be the next day. My disposition helped me ease quickly into the meditation and observation of my breathing and sensations. What seemed like torture when we started our Vipassana practice, to sit perfectly still for an hour and focus on our breathing and sensations, now felt easier. When Goenka's chanting marked the end of a session, I was surprised that the hour had already passed.

Milling about in the dining hall between the meditation and our evening discourse, I listened to stories the other women told of their experiences and of their lives. Again, I found myself enjoying the quiet contentment of being an observer, only asking a question here and there. Along with the sense of serenity I felt compelled to be moving so I donned my winter gear and braved the frigid outdoors.

The temperature had moderated a bit from the deep freeze it had been for most of the week, and I trekked out to wander the path on the perimeter. The air was cool and refreshing. I noticed the light was fading fast, and I could see the yard lights of a neighbouring farm in the distance flicker on. Turning toward the house, the interior lights had been turned on, and I could make out silhouettes of the participants as they moved about on the main floor. Listening for sounds, I heard several dogs barking in the area, and in the distance the sounds of cars rushing by on the highway. I hadn't noticed any of these things earlier in the week, and I felt that not only had I made discoveries about me, I was more aware of my surroundings. I made a mental note of the feeling of peace and happiness, not as something to crave and long for, instead just by being in the moment and noticing what I was seeing, hearing, and sensing. I stopped for a few minutes and as I did I felt a flush of warmth start at the top of my head and move down my body as though it was cloaking me. I smiled and returned to the house just before we retreated to the meditation hall for the evening discourse.

Climbing onto the tower of comfort, I wrapped myself in the blue flannel blanket that had provided me with warmth and security and settled in for Goenka's final teachings. "The tenth day is over and come 7:30 tomorrow morning you have come to the end of this seminar so this evening, let us review." I enjoyed the way that Goenka spoke; his accent and how he structured his sentences made for an interesting lecture. Every evening for the past ten, he had entertained our group with stories and educated us with wisdom and charmed me with his charismatic style. I felt a little down that the retreat would soon be over. That feeling of melancholy passed almost as quickly as it had come as I tuned in to our last discourse.

A smile spread on my face as Goenka delved into the overview, reminding us that when we first came to the course we took refuge in the tradition of Buddha's teachings which meant one who is fully enlightened. He emphasized that this was a study in the law of nature and was universal, not a religious practice, and as we returned home, dhamma as he called it, was very important. "Take refuge in yourself, make the island of yourself. Develop dhamma within yourself and this dhamma will be your real refuge."

I had come here to discover the secret to happiness and realized that I create my own reality so the power and tools I needed were found by turning inward, making myself my own safe harbour. Goenka identified two yardsticks to measure our progress on the path: the first was service to others without expecting anything in return: and, second a feeling of gratitude. The emphasis on appreciation really caught my attention, and I remembered a practice I had started but let slip. When I kept a gratitude journal and each day wrote three things I was thankful for, I did feel better and made a mental note that it was time to resume that as a part of my self-care routine when I returned home.

Goenka reminded us that the Vipassana technique used no visualizations or verbalizations so that the focus could be completely on our natural breath. As we developed this awareness our minds became sharper. He described the ultimate truth of the solidified body as the tiny vibrations that we were able to feel as we sat in silence. Noticing the sensations and recognizing that they come and go showed me that there is always change. Not reacting to the sensations, simply noticing them was a challenge at first, but that was a huge part of the teachings to remain equanimous, neither craving nor having an aversion to the sensations.

I was moved when Goenka shared his personal story of discovering meditation. He struggled with stress and serious migraine headaches. He wanted to leave his retreat many times. He finished his story by saying, "When the mind is purified, the source of the pain goes away." I chuckled when he said, "But Vipassana is not just for migraines, it is for all the miseries of life." *How true is that!*

His closing statement touched my heart, and I felt tears well up in my eyes as he blessed us with, "Vipassana is a jewel. May all of you make use of this wonderful jewel and come out of the miseries—all the miseries. Enjoy real peace, real harmony, real happiness. Take rest, take rest, take rest."

The first inklings of fatigue seeped in as I climbed the stairs to the dining room. I said good night to a few people on the way to my room. Veronica was a few minutes behind me as she stayed to speak with her husband about their drive home. She came in the room as I was about to retire for the night, and she approached me and surprised me by giving me a quick embrace. "I know we are not supposed to touch, but I just want to thank you for staying. I was so worried you would leave. Thank you, thank you," she declared in her thick Portuguese accent.

Startled, I let out a giggle and said, "No problem." I wasn't sure what else to say. She turned, gathered her things, and went into the bathroom. I smiled, climbed onto my cot, and drifted quickly to sleep so I didn't even hear her climb into her bed sometime later.

Simple Steps to Reignite Your Happiness

Stir Your Soul | Do you reserve the words "I Love You" for special occasions? Rather than treating the words "I Love You" like your fine china that's used sparingly and carefully, consider them like your everyday dishes—caringly, but frequently put to good use.

Power Up Your Potential | Develop a relationship with silence. The power and tools you need are found by turning inward. You are your own safe harbour.

Activate Your Awareness | Acknowledge anger, regret and sadness about the person you've become that's so drastically different from who you wanted to be. Only then can you become that person you truly want to be.

Rock Your Resilience | Focus on something that you regret not ever doing up to this point in your life. Consider ways that you might be able to experience it in some fashion in the future.

Kick Ass With Intentional Action | Acknowledge someone out loud for something they've done that you really appreciate. Let them know how grateful you are and see how appreciation creates a connection.

Day Eleven

"If you feel lost, disappointed, hesitant, or weak, return to yourself, to who you are, here and now and when you get there, you will discover yourself, like a lotus flower in full bloom, even in a muddy pond, beautiful and strong."

Masaru Emoto, Secret Life of Water

"Tears welled up in my eyes and a few spilled down my left cheek, but it wasn't sadness that brought sniffles—it was a deep sense of gratitude for the life-changing experience. This marked the end of the retreat, but the beginning of a profound change in the way that I saw the world and myself in it."

Day 11

Reignite Your Excitement

It felt like Christmas morning. My eyes popped open, and I was ready to jump out of bed, eager to get the day started—and it was only 3:55 a.m. My heart raced with excitement about being done and going home! I quietly pushed the covers off and tiptoed to the bathroom, so I wouldn't wake Veronica with my earlier than normal rising.

"Good morning!" Crap. I nearly jumped out of my skin when Veronica spoke to me from her bed in the darkened room. I skittered towards my cot and jumped on it, banging my head on the wall with a corresponding "uumph."

The two of us giggled as she said, "Sorry, I didn't mean to scare you."

"No problem, I'm still adjusting to us being able to talk, and I didn't think you were awake yet." I stretched out on my bed, and we made small talk about our respective trips home. It was a bit like a teenagers' slumber party as we both laid in the dark talking. After about fifteen minutes, Veronica declared that she was going to meditate in the hall. I decided to pack my things and be ready to hit the road as soon as we were released.

The night before we had been asked to sign up for some pre-departure duties to assist the staff with clean up. When the work was first mentioned, I felt resistance as I was eager to leave, and this would delay my exit. I contemplated sitting back and waiting for others to step up, hoping that all the tasks would be completed. A twinge of guilt and sense of duty charged into my consciousness at the thought of not pitching in.

But that's the old me, doing things out of obligation, not considering my own needs, participating for fear that I would let someone down or not be liked if I didn't help out. Would it be selfish to request an exemption from the work? I could just announce to everyone that I have a huge day of driving ahead of me. For crying out loud, I haven't even left the retreat and already I am working myself into knots making a basic decision.

I closed my eyes, took a deep breath, stopped the chatter in my head and decided to just look at the list. While I perused the inventory of jobs, my attitude changed from obligation to contribution. For a life-changing experience, a little elbow grease was a small price to pay and participating in the efforts was a way to show my appreciation. I was startled that the shift in perspective was so swift. In the end, I volunteered to clean our ensuite and collect the perimeter ropes and stakes from the women's side of the yard. Those seemed like the quickest tasks to complete so I could embark on my nine-hour drive as soon as possible.

I had all of my belongings ready at the bedroom door and the necessary cleaning done as the gong rang for our final breakfast together. Pausing outside my room, I took a final look at the grand dining area below, watching both male and female participants drift in from different parts of the house. I expected to hear boisterous chatter and noise drift up to the second level, but I heard only the occasional "good morning" while people formed the line to dish up their food. The animated discussions during the afternoon before were absent. Walking down the stairs toward the group, I was aware of a subdued energy from the collective. I wondered if the other participants were easing into a change in routine, or if, like me, they were savouring the last of the serenity.

Just as I passed the pot of porridge, Sandy came up behind me and said, "Not going to miss this goop when I go home."

I laughed, turned my head to make eye contact, and with a grin said, "Amen, sister!" I grabbed only an apple and a cup of peppermint tea as I had plans to stop at the first Tim Hortons I found and indulge in a large coffee and breakfast sandwich—with meat.

Sandy and I found stools next to each other, and I made eye contact with a few around the table, nodding and saying good morning. It was a refreshing change to be able to acknowledge people both non-verbally and through vocal exchanges. Sandy continued to talk, but I was not paying attention to what she was saying, I was noticing that her entrance was the icebreaker that others used to start having conversations. I was happy to be quiet and absorb the sound of the dialogue around me just like the day before. However, that morning I also knew that some of that silence was because my thoughts were focused on leaving rather than simply being present.

Eating quickly, I grabbed my coat and ventured out in the dark to finish the last of my commitments. Fortunately, the milder weather had lingered, and it was refreshing, but not bitterly cold as I set about collecting the three-foot long stakes that had been placed in the ground and the twine that was strung between them.

A slight miscalculation about the ease of the task hit me as I sunk to my mid-thighs in a snow bank to reach the furthest stake. These were flimsy little pieces of wood that I thought I could pluck easily out of the ground, quickly wrap the twine and be on my way.

Wrong!

I don't know how they got them in there, but they weren't coming out easily. Standing in the deep snow, I stretched one arm to grab the wood and pulled up. The stake stayed put, and I lost my balance—landing face first in the snow. With three limbs buried in the snow, torso lying on top, and one arm flailing around trying to grab the stake to push myself up, I looked like I was drowning—the true picture of panic. I grabbed the stake, and it breaks. *Crap!*

The more I flailed, the deeper I sank into the snow. Unfortunately, it was still dark out, and without yard lights I knew I could not be seen from the house.

I wonder how long I would have to wait for someone to find me? Too long. I have to get out of this on my own. Great, I survive a ten-day silent meditation retreat only to freeze ass up and face down in a snow bank.

Having nothing solid to push against, all hopes of a graceful recovery were gone. With all the momentum I could muster, I threw my butt backwards as though I was preparing to sit on the toilet then flung my torso as though I was flopping on a bed. This was enough to rock me onto my backside. *At least now I'm face up and ass down.* For just a second, I caught my breath before rolling onto my side and pushing myself to an upright position, freeing my legs from the deep embankment. My clothes were soggy from my swim in the snow, and I surprised myself by starting to laugh. It started as a nervous guffaw at the relief of getting out of a tight spot, and then turned into a giggle at the vision of a very ungraceful dismount. Even though I was the only one to enjoy the spectacle, it put a smile on my face while I carried on.

Picking up the stick and wrapping the twine around it, I wandered to the next stake, grabbed it with both hands and with some effort pulled it out. Fortunately, the rest of the perimeter fence was along the path of beaten down snow so I had easier access, but most did not come out easily as they were frozen into the ground. Several sticks broke off as I was trying to extract them. Even though the temperatures had moderated, it was still too cold to be out long, especially with wet clothing. I worked as quickly as possible, and by the time I was finished, I was shivering. I entered the house, walked directly to my bags and grabbed my towel, dry clothes, and my toiletry bag before heading to the bathroom to get warm and dry. I debated about having a hot shower, but I was eager to collect my keys and get on the road.

As I passed the dining area, I noticed that many of the participants and staff still lingered around the breakfast table in no apparent rush to end their time there. I gathered up my keys and cell phone from the table and called out a collective farewell to the group where they sat. Most of the women responded with a smile, wave, and send off salutation. Melanie and Veronica got up from their seats to give me a hug good-bye.

I appreciated the kind gesture from my roommate, Veronica. Even though we had shared space for the last ten days, I did not feel a deep connection with her, but for the third time since we were able to speak, she put her hands on my shoulders and earnestly thanked me for staying. The first two times she mentioned it I brushed it off with a flippant comment. That last time I paused long enough to really take in the sentiment of her words.

"You are welcome, Veronica." I replied graciously, feeling humbled that I had a positive impact on her experience.

When Melanie hugged me, a lump rose in my throat. I swallowed to keep my emotions in check and the tears from flowing. A bond had been created between the two of us, and even though I was twenty years her senior, I felt a maternal nurturing vibe from her as she embraced me to say farewell. She was carrying on with her world travels, and I was continuing on a journey of my own. Our paths had crossed for a brief and profound moment. I was once again reminded of the poem, regarding people coming into our lives for a season, a reason, or a lifetime. When Rochelle left on day eight, I felt a sense of abandonment because I had no opportunity to say good-bye. With Melanie, there was no exchange of contact information or promises to stay in touch, and I was completely content with that decision. I gave her one extra squeeze and said simply, "Thank you." Unspoken understanding passed between us and a calm and pleasant sense of closure surrounded me.

Then I ducked back into the cold to see if my van would start after being idle in frigid temperatures for the last ten days. As

I opened the back door the cold metal hinges creaked and resisted movement from lack of use. Throwing my suitcase and giant black cushion into the back, the eagerness to get on the road was rising. I climbed in the driver's seat and held my breath, anxiously hoping that my vehicle would start. The engine groaned as it slowly turned over defiantly. It took a few of those cautious revolutions before it caught, and the motor sprang to life. I said a little prayer of gratitude that my battery held its charge without the block heater being plugged in for ten days. In that moment, I was prepared to do a testimonial for Ford Motor Company about the hardiness of their vehicles in the frigid Canadian temperatures.

As eager as I was to get on the road, the old van needed time to get the fluids running through her before I drove away. Reluctantly, I stepped back into the cold, and crossed the driveway to take refuge in the warmth of the house one last time.

While I waited for my vehicle to warm up, I stood in the grand foyer and leaned against the door, appreciating the beauty of the tall ceilings and the huge bonsai tree directly in front of me, as though I was taking a snapshot for my memory. I listened to the chatter drifting in from the dining area and smiled, thinking how quiet it had been when I arrived just ten days earlier as participants entered with varying levels of anticipation and anxiousness. A wave of emotion washed over me. Tears welled up in my eyes and a few spilled down my left cheek, but it wasn't sadness that brought sniffles—it was a deep sense of gratitude for the life-changing experience. This marked the end of the retreat, but the beginning of a profound change in the way that I saw the world and myself in it. With a deep breath, I walked out the door, excited to head home.

The ice on the windshield had defrosted, but there was still a chill to the air coming out of the vents. I knew that would change once I started driving and the engine had time to heat even further. The sun had not yet come up over the horizon, but the darkness of the night was starting to lighten enough that I could see the house.

With a final glance at my peaceful sanctuary, I put the vehicle into gear and slowly pulled away.

I drove for about five minutes through the small subdivision, admiring the beautiful huge houses along the way. At the first stop light I reached over and flipped on the radio. I expected I would have to tune it to find some upbeat music to celebrate my release from quiet camp and the start of an exciting journey toward my family, coffee, meat, and the holidays! Instead of cheerful tunes, the soulful crooning of Bing Crosby wafted out of my speakers as he sang, *"I'll Be Home for Christmas."* The tears that had earlier brimmed my lower lids were back again, accompanied this time by sobs. I didn't have a rational thought about what the emotion meant. I knew that I needed to allow it to flow freely and be released. I continued to cry for fifteen minutes, passing at least one Tim Hortons. The coffee was less important than whatever was happening to me in that moment. Eventually, the waterworks subsided, and I wiped my face. *Phew, now that's over with I can get on with the search for my steaming hot cup of brew.* By this time, I was on the divided highway and knew the desired establishment was at the next exit.

With my caffeine cravings met, I set about the next thing on my list. I picked up the cell phone and dialed my mom and dad's number. Dad answered with noticeable amusement in his voice, "Well hello, Stranger. I'm glad to hear your voice, although I did expect to hear it earlier than this."

We both laughed, acknowledging his tongue-in-cheek prediction that I would be kicked out on day three for talking. I can't wait to see his reaction when I tell him how I bent the rules! Yup, total rebel! "What are you guys having for lunch?" Enough of the small talk. Let's get down to business. Bring on the beef! I knew from experience that Mom always had her meals planned for the day and would have taken meat out of the freezer.

"Well, what do you want?" Dad asked.

"Mashed potatoes, peas, and hamburger," I said, salivating as I announced it.

"I could do a roast. There should be time." My dad had been doing all the cooking since Mom had taken a nasty plunge off a ladder, severely fracturing her ankle and leg. She was in a wheelchair, so he had become the domesticated caregiver—a role previously foreign to my dad, but one he had taken on with no complaints and pride in doing an amazing job.

"Thanks, Dad, but the hamburger is what I've been craving." As I said the words, Goenka's voice popped into my head reminding me that cravings and aversions caused misery. In this case, I was totally prepared to defy my sainted guru with deference to enjoy my childhood comfort foods. Dad and I approximated the time of my arrival and disconnected.

Before leaving the parking lot, I called Stew, but got the answering machine. I was a little deflated to hear my own voice click in to say, "Hi, thanks for calling the White house. We can't take your call right now." I had hoped to catch someone at home. Even though it had not been my practice to call my family while I was travelling for business, I longed to make a connection with Stewart or the kids. After calling his work and cell number, I finally conceded and left a message saying that I was on the road and expected to be home by early evening. I resisted the urge to comment on him not answering his cell phone, as I normally would have expressed frustration. *Wait a second. That's progress right there!* My initial reaction of disappointment was fleeting, and I smiled to myself as I recognized an opportunity to let it go and carry on.

The radio station continued to play Christmas music, and it put me in an even more festive mood. I cranked up the volume and started the trek north, singing along at the top of my lungs and even doing a little seat dancing along the way. Normally, driving was a time when I would be deep in thought, but I had had my fill of contemplation, so I chose to focus on the tunes.

I was content and happy, enjoying the music and the inner sense of peace that I felt.

As I approached my parents' home, dark clouds had formed in the north and big fluffy snowflakes were falling gently to the ground. I made a mental note not stay too long so the precipitation didn't have much time to accumulate and cover the roads. I called out as I entered through the garage and headed directly to the bathroom. When I emerged, Mom was waiting for me. I was giddy with excitement, and my earlier willingness to sit and listen as I returned to the land of communication was left in the dust. "Hi Mom!" I bent over and gave her a big hug and kiss before pushing her chair back into the kitchen.

"How was your trip?" she asked.

"I'll tell you all about it while we eat." *I do have priorities!* The room was filled with the delicious smell of home cooking, and Dad was heaping mounds of potatoes and bright green peas into the serving dishes. I salivated just at the thought of eating. *So much for no cravings!*

He came around the island to give me a hug before returning to his hosting duties. "You better eat quick and get on the road. Looks like the weather is going to stay for a bit." As farmers, my father and brothers were constantly aware of, analyzing, and discussing the weather.

As Mom and I made our way to the table, I shared the details of my grand adventure. Dad placed the serving dishes on the table, and I piled the vegetables on my plate, waiting for him to bring the crowning glory from the stove. It was as though I was in an episode of some famous chef show and the creator was about to glide in with a gloriously prepared and professionally presented fancy entree. Reality was much better. I was overjoyed to watch my dad in his work clothes—a button up western shirt and GWG blue jeans—pick up the frying pan from the cook top and approach the table. A little fanfare sound bite went off in my head, and I almost blurted, "doot to do do," as I watched the steam from the ground meat dish rise above the pan edges. He set it down in front of me, and I resisted the urge to push my plate to the side, dig my fork in and eat directly from the pan! I savoured the hamburger, prepared exactly as I loved it, with onions and a can of Campbell's mushroom soup to give it a creamy sauce. Closing my eyes, I let the flavour flood my taste buds before I even started to chew and swallow. That was the only two minutes of my entire visit where I was completely silent as I relished the first bites. When I opened my eyes, my parents were watching in quiet amusement, and I think my dad breathed his first sigh of relief that his little girl had not changed as much as he thought she was going to—she still loved her beef!

I continued to regale them with story after story of the teachings of Goenka, what the house was like, how I had met Rochelle, that she left, and other highlights of the experience. They laughed out loud as I recounted the details of me purging and getting to talk with Melanie.

I was so animated and expressive it was more like a presentation than a conversation, and they sat back and watched the show rather than asking questions or making comments. I was aware that I was hyped and gregarious, but it felt like a release of pent up positive energy. The ringing of the phone put my exuberant rant on hold for a moment while Dad got up to answer it. It was my brother Trevor, and when Dad told him I was there, he asked to speak to me. I took the hand set from Dad, and said, "Hey Trev, how you doing?" Nothing.

"Hello?"

Nothing,

"Did you hang it up? He's not there," I told Dad. Then I heard the snicker on the other end of the line.

"I'm here. I just thought you might be missing quiet camp, so I was giving you the silent treatment!" responded Trevor.

I laughed, and he asked how it was. "It was amazing." I could have delved into so much more detail but knew that I had to get on the road. We bantered back and forth for a few minutes then said our good-byes. Dad took the phone back and finished discussing farm business with Trevor.

I glanced outside and noticed that the snow fall was heavier than when I first arrived. "I'd better get on the road."

"Thanks for the visit. We are so happy you had a great time," Mom responded, affirming my decision to leave. I observed her as I finished the last of my tea. Despite being confined to the wheelchair, she appeared healthy and strong. A little out of character, she wore a baggy sweatshirt and stretchy pants, both for ease of dressing and to get the pant legs over the bulky splint and bandaging on her lower leg. She had run a brush through her short brown hair and she wore no makeup, but her skin was clear with nice pink coloring in her cheeks.

I bent over and gave Mom a kiss and a long embrace. There were so many thoughts that I wanted to share with her, about feeling emotionally abandoned, forgiveness, and acknowledging her with love and respect for doing her best. I had processed my relationships at the retreat and knew that I wanted a deeper connection, but I was not yet prepared to delve into a therapeutic dialogue, so I kept my parting comment brief.

"Love you."

She patted me on the back, "Good-bye, dear. Drive safe."

It did occur to me that my descriptions and stories were light and funny as though I was describing a fun vacation rather than a deep and profound spiritual experience. The time for discussions around my insights and healing could wait until another time. That was what felt appropriate and natural in the moment, yet I wondered if I was reverting to an old pattern of interacting at a very surface level. The energy of the visit was a whirlwind—I breezed in, talked incessantly, and made a hasty departure.

Dad hung up the phone, so he could walk me to the door. Before I hugged him, he placed his hands on my shoulders, looked me in the eye and said, "I'm glad you stopped in to tell us about the retreat. Have a safe trip, girlie."

I felt a little ache of emotion in the middle of my chest when he used the childhood term of endearment. I gave him a hug as the ache turned into a warm flow across my chest. I dismissed the concern about being disconnected; I was totally present and aware of my own response. *Besides, I learned that you can bond with no talking and no touch—and here I experienced both.* I appreciated the firm farewell squeeze and was pleased that I had stopped in, even if it was for only an hour and a half. It was important, *not just for the beef,* but also to share the highlights of my experience with mom and dad.

The large flakes melted on my cheeks, and my hair was instantly matted with snow as I walked across the yard to get in the van. I didn't have to brush off the vehicle as only a small amount of precipitation covered the windshield and the wipers took care of it easily. I honked and waved as I drove past the front of the house and saw Mom sitting in her chair, watching as I turned north onto the gravel.

The country roads were covered, but I was still able to make out the ditches so I wasn't worried as I glanced in the rear view mirror to see my tracks, obvious in the fresh fallen snow.

Turning onto the main highway, I noticed that the maintenance trucks had gone through and cleared the pavement. I was relieved that even though it was snowing, I anticipated decent winter driving conditions. That expectation could not have been more wrong, when thirty minutes into my trip the situation changed.

I was driving just below the speed limit when an impatient driver pulled out and passed me, creating a swirling cloud of fresh powder that momentarily blinded my view of the road.

"Jerk," I uttered under my breath. *Not so loving and equanimous now!*

Taking my foot off the gas was enough to slow down, and I resisted the instinct to touch the brake in case the road was slippery. As the other car forged ahead the gusts died down and so did the snow, improving the visibility. I loosened my grip on the steering wheel, stretched my hands as I realized how my whole body had tightened up. I took a deep breath. It didn't have the normal relaxing effect because just ahead, the vehicle that passed me suddenly disappeared. It was as though a white curtain had opened up, engulfed him, and then closed.

I reached down to make sure my lights were on as I too entered the intensity of a winter white out. This time I did touch the brakes as I couldn't see the taillights of the car I knew was somewhere in front of me. The ice fog was so thick it enveloped the van. I was in a bubble, moving slowly through it. My chest tightened with fear, and the tension I had tried to let go of minutes before returned with even more intensity.

My mind raced with options to safely escape the treacherous situation. I knew that stopping on the side of the highway put me at risk of being run into by a vehicle coming from behind. Besides, I wasn't exactly sure where the edge of the road was, and I knew that I had been driving into the river valley, so the deep ditches and bridge meant I didn't want to miscalculate and exit the hardtop. Turning around was out of the question. My only option was to keep moving forward—cautiously. I didn't need to look at my speedometer to know that I was only travelling at a crawl. I hoped that anyone approaching from behind would also have slowed down significantly. Suddenly, I was relieved that the car had passed, leading the way through the storm, and even though I couldn't see him, I felt more secure knowing he was ahead, so I could watch for him.

I leaned forward in my seat and placed my focus on the road just in front of the hood of the van. The base of the fog was about two feet off the ground, so I could make out the dark pavement, but if I looked at eye level all I saw was a wall of white. I took a deep breath to release some tension and concentrate on the small area of visibility that allowed me to move forward. I continued to watch for taillights and noticed I was scrunching my eyes as though it would help me see better. It didn't. I felt a small thud and change in the road noise and I knew that I was now on the bridge deck which meant I was at the lowest part of the valley and soon would be climbing up the other side, hopefully out of the fog and blinding snow. You're going to be fine. Just breathe and keep moving. *There's the other side of the bridge. You're doing great. What the hell is with the storms—one on the way to the retreat and now this?*

A second thump on the road told me I was across the bridge and knew from memory that the long climb out of the valley was just ahead. I felt the pitch of the van change, and I pushed the accelerator but maintained my snail's pace—*definitely going up.*

Just as suddenly as I had driven into the abyss, I popped out of the blinding whiteout as I crested the top of the hill. The ice fog was behind me and the flurries of snow were dwindling on the north side of the gorge. Only ten minutes up the road the weather changed dramatically, relief flooding through me as the skies cleared, and the sun peaked out from the clouds. The tension slowly released, and I shifted in my seat to shake off the last of it.

Fortunately, the next five hours of driving were uneventful as the roads were clear and no precipitation complicated my winter trek. I took the opportunity with the good conditions to do some reflections about the retreat and the storm I had just driven through.

The intense weather mirrored my time at silent camp. Churning thoughts and emotions were present in the early days of meditation and not knowing what was ahead of me, I still pushed on. A sudden shift happened on day six when I dropped deeply into the valley of my feelings, I experienced blinding pain, purging, and uncertainty about what was ahead—knowing there was no stopping and certainly no turning back. I kept moving forward cautiously through the emotional and physical storm, only to come out clearer and lighter on the other side. Slowing down and taking each day, each hour, and sometimes each minute as it came, got me through the retreat.

Similarly, the ice fog and limited visibility had actually created the opportunity for me to be very present—aware of my surroundings, conscious of my reaction and intent on proceeding. Rather than turning back or stopping, the only way to conquer the storm was to go through it. Fortunately, the outcome was positive!

Wow, I still haven't learned to slow down. It took a treacherous situation to get me to stop forging ahead like a sugared-up toddler in a toy store. Why the hell was I on the road anyway? Why hadn't I decided to stay at Mom and Dads until the conditions were better?

In a familiar trend, I had disregarded what was happening all around me in deference to making it home as soon as possible. In fact, all three of us had acknowledged the weather, but it never occurred to me, or to them, that I should stay put. Instead, I put myself in jeopardy. I had spent my life forging ahead, being fiercely independent, and trying to prove that I can succeed— even against Mother Nature! Had I slowed down, taken a breath and really considered the winter road conditions, I could have avoided the intense minutes and the potential of a disastrous outcome. It was obvious to me that I still needed to learn when to stop or pause, and when to slowly move forward or surge ahead.

Proceeding north toward my home in Fort McMurray, the light of the day was fading, and I decided I had enough of contemplation and serious concentration. I turned the tunes up to enjoy Christmas music for the last few hours of my drive. There were no towns, just the dark wilderness so I was happy to see the lights come into sight as I reached city limits. Following the highway around the bend into the river valley, I had a nostalgic moment, appreciating the downtown vista with the familiar Christmas trees lit up in Lion's Park on the right and our little neighbourhood visible along the river to the left. The multi-coloured holiday lights added to my festive mood.

Yet, my excitement about being home was mixed with apprehension. Returning to familiar surroundings and my loved ones, I questioned if I could sustain the positive changes I had experienced. In the midst of the outer chaos of my life, I would need to be vigilant to maintain the inner tranquility of peace and happiness.

I paused in the driveway, appreciating the holiday decorations and enjoyed one last moment of quiet. I usually teased Stew about the amount of Christmas lights he adorned the house with, likening him to Clark Grizwald in *National Lampoon's Christmas Vacation,* but that night I thought it was absolutely beautiful.

As I was collecting my belongings out of the back of the van, the front door opened and Stew called, "Do you need help?"

"No, I got it thanks." *That's different! Maybe he's glad to see me! And there's that streak of fierce independence again! Why didn't I accept his help?*

I balanced the load and headed towards the warmth of my home. As I stepped past Stew into the house, I gave him a quick kiss before setting everything down in the front entry. Sianna was the first to come bounding down the stairs, "Hi, Mama! How was everything?"

I took her into my arms and kissed her head, "It was great. How are you?"

"Fine, I'm glad you're home." A warm wave flushed from the lump in my throat down toward my chest and settled on my heart.

The twins waited to greet me. Shaelyn gave me a peck on the lips and a quick embrace happily chirping, "Hi, Mama," before moving aside to let Rylee in for a longer hug.

"Hi Mom." He didn't say more, but held on longer than the girls, neither of us rushing to end the moment of connection. *When did they get so grown up?*

Stew carried my bags upstairs while the kids caught me up on what had happened at home. I sat on the couch and our dog, Bandit, promptly jumped on my lap to cuddle, showing he was happy to have me back. For twenty animated minutes, I listened as the kids talked about what was happening in their lives. I was completely content to listen, and happy that none of them asked for details about my experience because there was too much to tell and I didn't know where to start.

With a simple check-in with myself, I acknowledged that I was exhausted. I had been up since before four am and it was nearly my regular retreat bedtime. After the kids shared their lives with me they were satisfied to return to their rooms and get ready for bed.

I moved over to where Stew had settled on the couch.

"So it was good?"

"Yeah, it was really amazing and worth every minute. I'll tell you about it tomorrow."

"I'm glad you're home." He put his arm around my shoulder to give me a hug, and I snuggled in a little closer.

"I'm glad, too."

We sat for a few minutes more in silence. It was difficult to express what my experience was like; there was too much to be said—definitely more than one conversation's worth. Besides, I was still processing it myself. I discovered that even though I spent ten days connecting with myself and reflecting on my relationships, it was going to take some time to renegotiate how I showed up with people. Stepping away from the sacred space of the retreat, I needed time to ease back in and reframe my life from a different perspective. *Maybe I have learned something about slowing down?*

I gave Stew a kiss goodnight before climbing the stairs to our room. Crawling into my own comfortable king-sized bed was total luxury, and I snuggled under the sheet and thick down duvet. As I turned off the lights, I embraced real peace, real happiness, and real harmony.

Simple Steps to Reignite Your Excitement

Stir Your Soul | Recall a past accomplishment and the happiness you felt when you completed it. Bask in the afterglow of that achievement once again now. Really feel the sense of achievement and happiness.

Power Up Your Potential | When honouring a commitment, change your attitude from obligation to contribution. This simple mindset adjustment changes everything.

Activate Your Awareness | Pause and *really* allow it in when someone compliments or thanks you. Rather than brushing it off, explaining it away or saying, "It was nothing", try a simple, gracious "You're welcome".

Rock Your Resilience | Consider one area of your life where you need to slow down. Resolve to cut back on one activity that you feel is keeping you from being able to do something else that you *really* want to do.

Kick Ass With Intentional Action | Remember that friends enter your life for a season, a reason, or a lifetime. Take a moment to appreciate and feel gratitude for all of the various friendships you've experienced in your life.

Epilogue

"Sometimes all you have to do is show up and pay attention and your music happens."

Wayne Dyer, The Shift

"The impact that those ten days had on me was profound; however, the change was not immediate, and the teachings continue to echo as I continue on the path."

Epilogue

Laughing, Loving and Letting Go

It's been over a year and a half since I participated in the Vipassana retreat. That time has been filled with milestones and memories. Stewart turning fifty was certainly something to celebrate, and with the help of friends I planned an epic *Amazingly Adequate Race* based on the TV show. It was a huge success, and I was thrilled. *Of course, I now have established the standard for the 50th he will be planning for me.* During the evening party Stew shared his gratitude and graciously summed up the evening by saying, "These are the great moments in life—and it's important to pay attention." His sentiment had an impact on me as I was learning to have a deeper awareness of my own life experience well beyond the retreat. Shut up camp was intended to be a place where I would find answers. I was searching for happiness and fulfillment, as though they were prizes to be found at the end of a treasure hunt.

Looking back, I would say it was less of a discovery and more of an awakening. Like coming out of a deep sleep, slowly opening my eyes, drifting back into slumber, then gradually and gently becoming alert. The impact that those ten days had on me was profound; however, the change was not immediate, and the teachings continue to echo as I remain on the path.

The lessons I needed to learn were not intellectual, rather they were a connection to my heart and an allowing of deep emotions. For most of my life I worked hard to be strong, in control, and be the thinker. I now embrace the more loving, softer, gentler me—the one that is comfortable with vulnerability. Sometimes those feelings take me on a pretty wild ride; however, I feel more prepared to handle them.

When I dropped the struggle to be in control and always on top of things, relief set in, creating a sense of peace and contentment. Those sentiments showed up at various times. During a party to honour my parent's fiftieth wedding anniversary, I proposed a toast and spoke about the legacy of love that my parents had created together.

And, yes, I cried.

Driving home from the amazing weekend, Stew asked me who had acknowledged my speech at the party. I reflected for a moment then told him, "It was nice of people to comment, and I appreciated their gesture, but for one of the first times in my life it didn't matter what anyone thought. I am completely content with what I said and how I expressed it."

I was truly happy. For months I rode the surge of peace and joy I was experiencing as I worked on being present and cherishing the moments. Then there was a change.

When tragedy strikes us, grief becomes like a black cloud over everything, and we often lose sight of what makes us happy. What started out as a joyful family ski vacation quickly turned into a terrible nightmare when my thirteen-year-old niece, Cassidy, was tobogganing with her cousins and slid head first into a slab fence. In an instant, our world changed. The hours that followed were filled with gut wrenching terror and numbing disbelief. The neurologist at the Pediatric Intensive Care Unit confirmed that her multiple injuries and catastrophic head injury meant that we would need to say good-bye—too soon.

On Christmas morning, our family and close friends gathered for a final farewell. It was agonizing as we took turns individually, and in groups to talk, to hug, and to cry. The most powerful moment was when the entire family joined hands, created a circle around her bed, and spoke in unison, "We love you, Cassidy!"

On December 26, 2014 Cassidy Victoria Crisp became our forever Christmas Angel.

Heartbreak, once again, struck our family, and I was catapulted into the deep pit of grief, daily trying to claw my way out. Even equipped with experience and processing methods, it was difficult to maneuver through the emotional quagmire of anger, sadness, and profound loss. Yet,

I knew this was good. Instead of suppressing my emotions as I did after my brother Dale's death, I embraced them. I even noticed a difference with my parents. We spoke openly about the tragedy. Both my parents expressed their feelings to me, and I did what I could to support them in their grief.

Months after the accident, still working through my own thoughts and emotions, I realized that I continued to carry sorrow and heartache for my whole family, especially for my brother Charles and my sister-in-law Kelly. More than anything I wanted to ease their pain and heartache, and yet, I knew that I could not. Everyone's healing would happen in their own time and their own way.

Letting go of the grief created lightness in my disposition. The photos and videos that

Kelly shares on Facebook, filled with goofy faces, silly actions and giggles, remind me that Cassidy was the epitome of joy, love, and laughter—I'm grateful for the time she was with us.

It is in the saddest of times that I have needed to call on my courageous heart to assist me on this journey. Loss of loved ones, my struggle with depression, toxic thoughts and beliefs were phases requiring a tenacious fortitude.

On my search for happiness, these events were all part of the experience of life—*It's not good or bad, it just is*—and my heart led the way.

Each time I needed to reignite my own spark, I returned to the simple steps and lessons:

S - Stir Your Soul – I open up my heart, mind and soul to beauty and inspiration around me. There's so much for which to be grateful, all I need to do is open up and let it in.

P - Power Up Your Potential – I seek out methods and techniques for increasing my effectiveness and my results. No matter what I'm trying to do, someone has gone before me and I can learn from them.

A - Activate Your Awareness – Through meditation and introspection, I become aware of the emotions that flow through me and the thoughts that create those emotions. I allow the emotions, letting them follow their natural lifecycle, rather than trying to ignore or suppress them.

R - Rock Your Resilience – When challenges come up as they do, I acknowledge and embrace them as opportunities to grow. Profound transformation and personal growth occur through overcoming obstacles.

K - Kick Ass With Intentional Action – I focus my actions on what I'm intending to create in my life. Instead of simply being "busy", I move more quickly towards my dreams when my actions are deliberate and inspired.

What I have learned is that healing from burn out and grief will continue. Many deep conversations with my mom and dad about my own discoveries and understandings have brought us closer than I could have imagined. They have both been generous with their love and support, and I am very grateful.

My relationship with myself improves as well. Being more compassionate and accepting of who I am, reflects in my relationships with Stewart and the kids. I have not shared all the details of my personal growth with Stew; however, I am more honest about expressing my feelings, and delighted with the deepening intimacy of our marriage. We make a fantastic team— the thinker and the feeler—collaborating to create our own legacy of love.

I have changed as a parent. My attention has moved away from the physical care-giving and into the emotional well-being of my children. Admittedly, the kids are not as dependent on me as they once were. *In fact, sometimes they just don't need me at all!* We have talked about their childhood, and I have apologized for the unhappy person I was. The regret has diminished, and now I focus on being a positive role model for my children. The greatest act of love has been to allow them to be who they are, learn their own lessons, and be in a relationship of unconditional support. My desire is that Sianna, Shaelyn, and Rylee will always feel the profound pride and total admiration I have for them. "I love you," is spoken often, and I revel in the moments when I get the opportunity for a hug, a snuggle on the couch, or just hanging out and having a few laughs.

As I reconnect with old friends to reminisce and make new memories, I am reminded of the vast circle of love that extends beyond my family. My heart has once again opened up, so I am able to receive it. Yet, I know it is the relationship I have with myself that has the greatest influence on that receptivity.

I am the only person who can do this journey. I have mentors and guides; however, I've learned that I cannot rely on others to do my work for me. I've spent many hours attaining clarity by reading inspirational books, but I found my answers when I sat quietly and tuned into my own thoughts. And one of the things I discovered about myself was a connection to my inner comedian. I found my funny bone.

It was on day three of the retreat that I first became aware I was missing fun and laughter in my life. It was an early awakening that I didn't pay much attention to at first. Yet over time, as I stopped taking myself so seriously, I introduced funny stories and lightheartedness into my corporate workshops. Then my friend, Janene, noticed the change in my disposition and called to invite me to participate in a *Stand Up for Mental Health* show. While I didn't consider myself someone who still struggled with depression, I knew this was an opportunity to embrace and share the laughter that was inside me. I was merely waiting for a platform—*or a stage!*

Within weeks, I found myself studying under the tutelage of a professional comedian, along with six other volunteers, learning the fine art of stand-up comedy. I felt like I was in my natural element and was so excited about the opportunity. The day of the show, I reveled in the diva delights of having my hair and makeup professionally done. I connected with the other comedians through laughter and our collective nervousness about performing. And then, I went on stage and was myself—scripted yes, but not an act where I was pretending to be someone other than the goofy, sometimes messed-up woman that I am. It was liberating to poke fun at myself. *Actually, Stew was the key of many jokes, but he knew I was just kidding—mostly.*

Once uncovered, opportunities to nurture my comedic aspirations continued. I was invited to collaborate with twenty-three female authors from around the world to write *Success University for Women™*. My chapter titled, "What's so Funny about Success?" shares tips and strategies for laughter and fun—both of which I am thrilled I now have in abundance. And, once that comedy spark was reignited in me, it led me to launch my own show… *Shut the F*#% Up: Confessions of an Angry Housewife!*

In reality, my life has not changed, my perspective has. When I wake in the mornings—*well past four a.m.*—I take a moment to be grateful and allow the sensation of happiness to seep into my soul. To be truthful, that emotion doesn't always last through the day, sometimes not even past my morning cup of coffee. I still experience anger, sadness, resentment, and moments of judgment. There are times when the chatter of my inner bully becomes deafening.

Yet one thing has changed.

Whether it takes a moment, minutes, or a day, the key to my happiness and peace is to show up for myself—Let go of what does not serve me, embrace Love, and find the Laughter—to

Reignite My Spark!

About the Author

Carla White

With more than three decades of experience as a consultant, facilitator and yes, one of the first female Emergency Services Firefighters, **Carla White** earned her badassery badge by rising from the ashes of life's literal and figurative fires. Today, she's on a mission to educate, empower and inspire others to STOP letting life's inevitable fires burn them to the ground and START reigniting their own SPARK. From burnout and depression during her nursing career, to specializing in dealing with crisis and chaos in her work with clients, and surviving the 2016 Fort McMurray wildfire—Canada's largest and most expensive natural disaster in history—Carla knows a thing or two about bouncing forward from life's rock bottom moments. She applies her real-world expertise to consult with government agencies, municipalities, first responders and health care on their unique resiliency issues.

Carla is a 3x International Best-selling Author, including her featured story in *Chicken Soup for the Soul: The Spirit of Canada.*

Additionally, Carla is a sought-after consultant for human resource departments on crisis management and has worked with some of the world's top thought leaders as a Human Potential mentor and facilitator. In both capacities, Carla delivers leading edge content and mastery programs in Resiliency, Reinvention, Stress and Crisis Management.

As a keynote presenter and dynamic speaker, Carla brings a relatable, results- driven wit and charm to her exceptional storytelling. From seminars and strategic work sessions to executive retreats, Carla partners with you to **re-energize** your teams, **empower** your groups, and be a **catalyst for high impact change.**

Through her signature set of Resiliency Tools, Carla successfully shifts individuals and audiences around the world from stuck and stressed to refueled and reignited! Part powerful mindset practices, part life and business skill building, Carla's uncanny ability to transform audiences with her unique fusion of heart, humour and high impact content is unparalleled.

Dedication

With Gratitude

For the people I've met, the experiences I have had, and the tremendous opportunities to learn deeply, to open up to love, and to laugh again—the kind of laughter that lightens your soul. Special thanks to the gracious and loving human beings that have played a special role in both my personal journey and bringing this book to the world:

To Jack Canfield, Patty Aubrey and the entire Canfield family for the guidance, grace and acceptance, believing in me before I believed in myself. I am deeply grateful to Jack for being the inspiration to follow my dreams and for writing the Foreword.

To Kathy Sparrow, my writing coach, mentor, and friend. Thank you for helping me find my voice, edit and shape the narrative and hold space for me to develop into an author. Your devotion to the project and support through the cathartic process has been a beautiful gift.

To the beta readers who agreed to review the manuscript and provide feedback and testimonials, gracias mi amigos: Annabelle Bignell, Glenn Buchanon, Tina Burden, Milisa Burns, Emma Clewes, Angela Davis, Tracey Feist, Aleaha Frigon, Melody Hurtubise, Lacee Jacobs, Pamela Kathol, Roger King, Miriam Laundry, Sabrina Mattern, Donna Moore, Danne Reed, Jo-Anne Richardson, Lisa Russell, Hal Simonson, Zina Sokorinski, Daniel Sokorinski, Denise Stevenson, Russell Thomas, Kelly Tuohey, and Mike Vukelic.

To my Soul Sister, Danne Reed (from Kansas): There are a thousand reasons to give special mention to you…from sharing a brain to sharing some pain, you have been by my side through the entire journey and were instrumental in the final editing, revisions, and wisdom to get this book published and out to the

With Gratitude

world. The printing of this book means a chapter is closing. Fortunately, there is a whole book(s), tour, and life ahead to 'Show Up' with you by my side as Executive Producer, Business Partner, Dream Raiser and part of my Soul. Xoxo

I feel blessed to have been born in to a loving family. Immense gratitude to my parents, Terry and Dianne Crisp for their guidance, love, and support always! To my siblings, Denise (Nelson), Trevor (Sally), and Charles (Kelly) and my nieces and nephews, thank you for the amazing memories and moments that we have and will continue to create together.

To my children, Sianna, Rylee, and Shaelyn: Watching you grow into the extraordinary individuals you are has been the greatest gift of my life. Each in your own way, has inspired me to be a better person. I love you always and forever!

To Stewart White: This life adventure with you has been messy, playful, fun, challenging, funny, troubling, exciting, scary, rewarding, expanding, enriching and EPIC!! The whole time you have been at my side, as my greatest teacher, supporter and partner (even when I made it not so fun). Infinite gratitude and love—for all of it! I love you profoundly. xoxo

32431371R00150

Made in the USA
Columbia, SC
12 November 2018